# A-Z ISLE OF WIGHT
# VISITORS' ATLAS & GUIDE

## CONTENTS

Freshwater Bay

**Geographers' A-Z Map Company Limited**

Head Office : Fairfield Road, Borough Green, Sevenoaks, Kent TN15 8PP  Telephone: 01732 781000 (General Enquiries & Trade Sales)
Showrooms : 44 Gray's Inn Road, London WC1X 8HX  Telephone: 020 7440 9500 (Retail Sales)
www.a-zmaps.co.uk

Carisbrooke Castle

**The Isle of Wight's coat of arm bears the motto: 'All this beauty is of God'.**

The smallest county in the country after Rutland, the Isle of Wight lies off the south coast of England, bordered by the Solent and Spithead to the north and the English Channel to the south. Diamond shaped, it is 23 miles from east to west and 13.25 miles from north to south, and has an area of approximately 147 square miles (38,100 ha.) including inland water (enough for two thirds of the world's population!), with a coastline of 57 miles (92 km). The three main rivers, the Medina and the eastern and western River Yar all drain into the Solent and Spithead, the area around Freshwater west of the western River Yar being almost a separate island. The backbone of the Island is formed from a ridge of high chalk downland that runs from east to west between Culver Cliff and Tennyson Down whilst the highest point at 241 m (791 ft) is St Boniface Down near Ventnor. The diverse, and in places spectacular, landscape, exemplified by the rolling chalk downland, high chalk and sandstone cliffs, woodland, river estuaries, marshland, saltings and dunes together with coastal rock ledges and predominantly sandy beaches, has led to the Island being described as 'England in Miniature'.

In recognition of its beauty, almost half the Island's coast is designated as 'Heritage Coast'- and nearly half of the Island is designated an Area of Outstanding Natural Beauty, best appreciated from the Island's nine long distance paths or over 500 miles of bridleways and footpaths.

Newport, situated in the geographical centre is the Island's capital (the exact centre being at Shide Corner on the southern outskirts), however Ryde is the largest town whilst the best known internationally is undoubtedly Cowes with its many yachting events. Brighstone, Calbourne, Godshill, Shalfleet, Shanklin Old Village and Shorwell are some of the most picturesque of the villages. The Island has one of the best climates in the British Isles with resorts on the south-east coast receiving some of the longest hours of sunshine in Britain; it is also known for mild winter weather.

The Isle of Wight has a long history. Populated in Neolithic times, long barrow (communal burial mound) remains are evidenced by sites such as The Long Stone at Mottistone and Tennyson Down Mortuary Enclosure. Many Bronze Age round barrows (described as tumuli) dating from c.1900 BC can be seen, especially on the chalk downland of Afton, Mottistone and Brighstone Downs and at Headon Warren. After the invasion of Britain in 43 AD, the Romans named the Island 'Vectis', becoming an important trade route and using Brading Harbour as the main port. Villas have been excavated at several locations including one now covered up at Robin Hill, and Carisbrooke Castle is thought to be the site of a Roman fort. The Island was subject to constant French raids from the 14th to the 16th centuries, especially in 1377. In the 16th century Henry VIII instigated the building of a number of coastal defences which helped repel the last French invasion attempt in 1545. In the 1850s and 1860s refortification was undertaken at great expense under the Palmerston initiative to guard again the threat of a further French invasion but not a shot was fired in anger.

In Victorian times the Island became very fashionable and underwent a major influx of population with the development of many small villages into coastal resorts. The residency of Queen Victoria at Osborne House in 1846 only heightened this popularity. Easier access was afforded by the construction of the first railway line in 1862, later built into a complete network by 1900, at a time when road communication was poor. Steam ship services from the mainland also operated to many of the newly built piers. Queen Victoria is not the only royal associated with the Island as in 1647-48 King Charles I was imprisoned in Carisbrooke Castle shortly before his execution.

The Isle of Wight was notorious for shipwrecks, especially along the south-west coast colloquially known as the 'Back of the Wight', and many ships (nearly 300 recorded) have floundered on its shores. The most notorious location was Atherfield Point. The best known wreck is 'The Clarendon', a sailing ship which was driven ashore in huge seas off Blackgang in 1836. The remoteness of this southern coast meant that smuggling was rife, reaching its peak in the 18th century.

Alum Bay

The Island is noted for is red squirrel population, one of the last bastions in the south of England (the best place to see them is Parkhurst Forest), and is also notable for its rare species of fritillary butterflies.

An increasingly popular term for describing the Isle of Wight is 'Dinosaur Island' because of the amount of dinosaur fossils found in a layer of freshwater deposits from the Wealden Beds of the lower Cretaceous geological period exposed on the southern edge of the Island. Complete skeletons are a rarity, but in the 1990s three important, near-complete dinosaurs were discovered. Many of the finds have been at Compton, Brook and Brighstone Bays.

## Heritage Coast & Area of Outstanding Natural Beauty

The Isle of Wight has two designated Heritage Coasts, a classification given to coastlines in England and Wales which are of the highest quality and unspoilt nature. The Hamstead Heritage Coast stretches from Bouldnor to Gurnard Ledge on the north-west coast whilst the Tennyson Heritage Coast stretches from Totland Bay around The Needles headland, along the
south-west coast and around St Catherine's Point to Woody Bay, St Lawrence. The Isle of Wight Area of Outstanding Natural Beauty covers the entire south-west quarter of the Island from Newport, the western River Yar estuary to Yarmouth, the area around Newtown Bay in the north-west, the Osborne House estate in the north-east, an area of downland centred around Arreton Down and Ashey Down extending to Culver Cliff and Foreland, and the downs above Ventnor and St Lawrence in the south-east.

## Chines

'Chine' originates from the Saxon word 'Cinan' meaning a gap or yawn. Chines are formed by the rapid erosion of a cliff face by a river or stream, the effect being most pronounced when the cliff is made of soft clay or sand. The stream cuts down into the cliff whilst the face is worn back by the sea resulting in even more vigorous downward erosion. When not marred by landslides, the result is a narrow gully with steep sides. Although not unique to the Isle of Wight, chines are a characteristic of much of the cliffs of the Island's south-west and south-east coastline. Some, especially on the south-west coast, are fairly barren whilst others are rich in vegetation. Good examples can be seen at Blackgang Chine, Shepherd's Chine and Whale Chine (on the south-west coast), and Shanklin Chine and Luccombe Chine (on the south-east coast).

Luccombe Down

## FERRIES

Six ferry routes link from the mainland operating just over 400 crossings a day to and from the Island in the summer season. Turn up and go is available, but at peak season busy periods it is advisable to book in advance. Crossing times (which do not include queuing, loading and unloading) and service frequency listed below are approximate and are subject to change. Please check with the ferry operator before making your journey.

### Cowes (west)-East Cowes

Cowes Floating Bridge. Chain Ferry. 5 minutes (vehicular and foot passengers)
Frequent service between approximately 5am-12 midnight (Monday-Saturday), 7am-12 midnight (Sunday) from Cowes (Medina Road) to East Cowes (Bridge Square) over the River Medina. The next nearest bridge is at Newport. Service is subject to tides, weather and navigation demands.
Enquiries Tel: 01983 293041.

### Lymington-Yarmouth

Wightlink. Ferry. 30 minutes (vehicular & foot passengers)
Half hourly service (mid April-December), hourly (January-mid April) from Lymington (Lymington Pier station, east of Lymington River on Undershore, Walhampton) to Yarmouth (Bridge Road).
Enquiries Tel: 0870 5827744. www.wightlink.co.uk

### Portsmouth-Fishbourne

Wightlink. Ferry. 35 minutes (vehicular and foot passengers)
Half hourly service (mid April-December), hourly (January-mid April) from Portsmouth (Docks, Gunwharf Road) to Fishbourne (Fishbourne Lane).
Enquiries Tel: 0870 5827744. www.wightlink.co.uk

### Portsmouth Harbour-Ryde Pier Head

Wightlink. Catamaran Fastcat Service. 15 minutes (foot passengers only)
Half hourly service (mid April-December), hourly (January-mid April) from Portsmouth (near Portsmouth Harbour station, The Hard) to Ryde Pier Head (end of Ryde Pier, Esplanade).
There is no adjacent parking at Portsmouth, follow signs to city car parks. Pay and display parking is available at Ryde adjacent to the hovercraft terminal at the foot of the pier.
Enquiries Tel: 0870 5827744. www.wightlink.co.uk

### Southampton-Cowes (west)

Red Funnel. Catamaran Red Jet Hi-Speed Service. 22 minutes (foot passengers only)
Half hourly service (All year) from Southampton (Terminal 2, Town Quay) to Cowes (Red Funnel Pontoon, The Arcade).

Car parking is available at Southampton at Town Quay Triangle car park off Platform Road to the south-east of the terminal. There is no adjacent parking at Cowes, follow signs to town car parks.
Enquiries Tel: 023 80334010. www.redfunnel.co.uk

### Southampton-East Cowes

Red Funnel. Ferry. 55 minutes (vehicular and foot passengers)
Hourly service (March-December), hour and a half service (January-February) from Southampton (Terminal 1, Town Quay) to East Cowes (Red Funnel Pontoon, Trinity Road). Enquiries Tel: 023 80334010. www.redfunnel.co.uk

### Southsea-Ryde

Hovertravel. Hovercraft. 10 minutes (foot passengers only)
Half hourly service (All year) from Southsea Hoverport (Clarence Esplanade, Southsea seafront, immediately east of Clarence Pier) to Ryde Hovercraft Terminal (Esplanade, Ryde seafront, immediately east of Ryde Pier).

Pay and display parking is available at Southsea opposite the hoverport and along the sea front. Pay and display parking is available at Ryde adjacent to the terminal.
A 'hoverbus' service operates from Portsmouth shopping centre at Edinburgh Road, and Portsmouth and Southsea railway station at Isambard Brunel Road.
Enquiries Tel: 01983 811000 (Ryde), 023 92811000 (Southsea). www.hovertravel.co.uk

Operated since 1965 the service is now provided by two modern 98 seat AP1-88 hovercraft constructed on the Isle of Wight. Permitted to run at 45 knots with passengers, and capable of 60 knots on a calm flat sea, the cessation of cross channel car carrying hovercraft services means that this is now the only place where a timetabled hovercraft journey can be experienced in Europe.

## BUSES

The Island is served by an excellent bus network operated by Southern Vectis (www.svoc.co.uk), the services running to every point on the Island. A free 'Bus Guide' leaflet (with main services summary and route map) or a full timetable booklet titled 'Getting Around the Isle of Wight' (with all services and route maps with large scale sections covering the Island towns), are available from either tourist information centres or Southern Vectis Travel Centres at Cowes (32 High Street), Newport (Bus station, South Street), Ryde (Bus station, Esplanade) and Shanklin (43-45 Regent Street). Enquiry line Tel: 01983 532373 (Monday-Saturday 9-5.30). The two publications are bi-annual with summer and winter timetables. The routes are also shown by numbers depicted on the main maps in this atlas, although note that the placement of the numbers does not denote a bus stop.

Of immediate interest to the visitor are the 'Island Explorer' buses (service 7 (clockwise) and 7A (anti-clockwise), usually in a distinctive blue colour) that circle the Island in both directions travelling through Ryde, Brading, Sandown, Shanklin, Wroxall, Ventnor, St Lawrence, Niton, Freshwater Bay, Freshwater, Totland, Alum Bay, Yarmouth, Newport and Wootton. A round trip takes 4 hours. In the summer vintage open top buses (operating service 42) dating from 1939 to the 1950s run from Yarmouth (bus station) to Alum Bay via Colwell Bay and Totland, with exclusive use of the one mile long National Trust road from Alum Bay to the Needles Battery (usually pedestrian only). Interchange with the Island Explorer service can be made at Alum Bay, Totland or

Brighstone

Yarmouth. In bad weather closed top buses may be substituted and the route terminated at Alum Bay; service 42 does not run between November and the end of March.

Two other summer only services are usually operated by open top buses, subject to weather conditions. A linear route (service 43) travels between Sandown (Esplanade) and Shanklin (Esplanade). The Ryde and Downland Tour (service 88, operated by Westbrook Travel. Tel: 01983 533844) travels a one-way circular route through Ryde, Havenstreet, Arreton, Newchurch, Ashey, Sandown, Brading and back to Ryde via Westridge.

## CYCLE ROUTES
There are over 200 miles of bridleways and byways on the Island and many quite country lanes. In addition to the three official routes summarised below (and delineated in this atlas), there are many published route guides detailing circular routes of varying lengths. Bicycles can be hired from outlets around the Island.

### Round-the-Island Cycle Route
62 mile circular cycle route around the Island permanently marked with distinctive blue and white signs in both directions. The route avoids busy roads where possible with a short 1.5 mile section from Freshwater (The Causeway) to Yarmouth (Station Road) following the former Freshwater, Yarmouth and Newport Railway line (closed in 1953) alongside the River Yar estuary. There are several small differences in the route depending on the direction of travel and two alternative courses (for use in either direction), one in Yarmouth and the other through west Cowes.

A leaflet with route directions is available from the Isle of Wight Council or tourist information centres on the Island.

### Cowes-Newport Cycleway
3 mile cycle route on course of the former Isle of Wight Central Railway (closed in 1966) on the west side of the River Medina. The route runs from Arctic Road, Cowes (signposted from Cowes floating bridge) to the top of River Way, Newport (car park).

### Shide-Blackwater Cycleway
1.25 mile cycle route on course of the former Isle of Wight Central Railway (closed in 1956) south of Newport. The route runs from Shide Corner, Shide Road, Shide to Blackwater following part of the route of the Stenbury Trail.

## TRAINS
Island Line (www.island-line.co.uk), the remnant of the Island's once extensive railway system electrified in 1967, runs for 8.5 miles from Ryde Pier Head, via Ryde Esplanade, Ryde St John's Road, Smallbrook Junction (access by rail only), Brading, Sandown and Lake to Shanklin. The service is operated by refurbished former London underground stock. Free Park and Ride to rail users is available at Shanklin, Sandown and Ryde St John's Road stations. Connection with the Isle of Wight Steam Railway is possible at Smallbrook Junction on operating days (Tel: 01983 884343 / 882204). Carriage of bicycles (maximum of 4 per train at the Shanklin end of the train) is permitted at the conductor's discretion. For full details of train services telephone National Rail Enquiries on 08457 484950 or Ryde Esplanade Ticket Office on 01983 562492 or direct on 1983 812591.

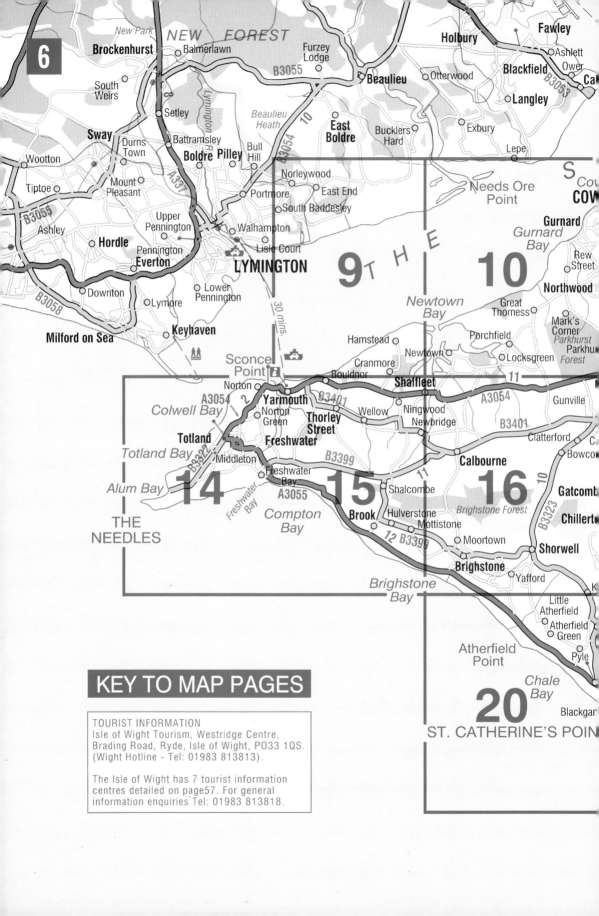

**6**

NEW FOREST

New Park
Brockenhurst
Balmerlawn
Furzey Lodge
South Weirs
Setley
Beaulieu
Holbury
Fawley
Ashlett
Ower
Blackfield
Langley
B3053
Ca
Otterwood
B3055
Sway
Durns Town
Battramsley
Boldre
Pilley
Bull Hill
Beaulieu Heath
East Boldre
Bucklers Hard
Exbury
Wootton
Mount Pleasant
Tiptoe
Upper Pennington
A337
B3054
10
Norleywood
Lepe
Needs Ore Point
S
Cow
COW
Ashley
Hordle
Pennington
Walhampton
Portmore
East End
South Baddesley
Gurnard
Gurnard Bay
Everton
Lisle Court
LYMINGTON
**9** T H E
**10**
Rew Street
Northwood
B3055
Downton
Lower Pennington
Newtown Bay
Great Thorness
Mark's Corner
Parkhu
Milford on Sea
Lymore
Keyhaven
30 mins.
Hamstead
Cranmore
Newtown
Porchfield
Locksgreen
Parkhurst Forest
B3058
Sconce Point
Norton
Yarmouth
Bouldnor
Shalfleet
11
A3054
Gunville
Colwell Bay
Norton Green
B3401
Thorley Street
Wellow
Ningwood
Newbridge
B3401
Clatterford
C
Totland
Freshwater
Bowco
Totland Bay
B3322
Middleton
B3399
Calbourne
10
Alum Bay
Freshwater Bay
**14**
Freshwater Bay
A3055
**15**
Shalcombe
**16**
Gatcomb
B3323
Chillert
THE NEEDLES
Compton Bay
Brook
Hulverstone
Mottistone
Brighstone Forest
Shorwell
12 B3399
Moortown
Yafford
Brighstone
Brighstone Bay
Little Atherfield
Atherfield Green
Pyle
Atherfield Point
Chale Bay
**20**
Blackgar
ST. CATHERINE'S POIN

## KEY TO MAP PAGES

TOURIST INFORMATION
Isle of Wight Tourism, Westridge Centre,
Brading Road, Ryde, Isle of Wight, PO33 1QS.
(Wight Hotline - Tel: 01983 813813).

The Isle of Wight has 7 tourist information
centres detailed on page57. For general
information enquiries Tel: 01983 813818.

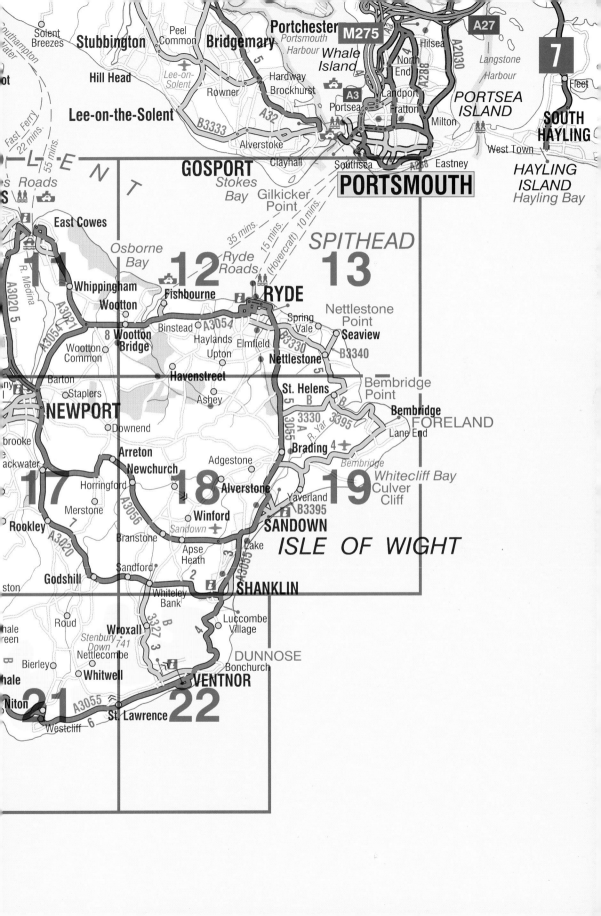

# REFERENCE

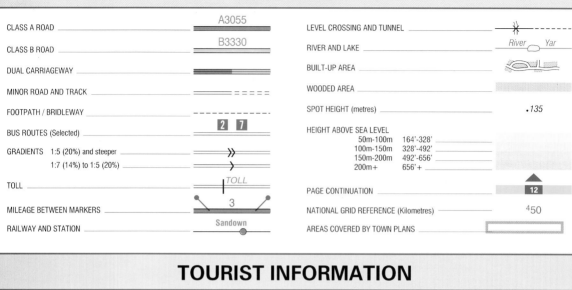

| | |
|---|---|
| CLASS A ROAD | A3055 |
| CLASS B ROAD | B3330 |
| DUAL CARRIAGEWAY | |
| MINOR ROAD AND TRACK | |
| FOOTPATH / BRIDLEWAY | |
| BUS ROUTES (Selected) | **2** **7** |
| GRADIENTS   1:5 (20%) and steeper | |
|             1:7 (14%) to 1:5 (20%) | |
| TOLL | TOLL |
| MILEAGE BETWEEN MARKERS | 3 |
| RAILWAY AND STATION | Sandown |

| | |
|---|---|
| LEVEL CROSSING AND TUNNEL | |
| RIVER AND LAKE | River      Yar |
| BUILT-UP AREA | |
| WOODED AREA | |
| SPOT HEIGHT (metres) | .135 |
| HEIGHT ABOVE SEA LEVEL | |
|   50m-100m    164'-328' | |
|   100m-150m   328'-492' | |
|   150m-200m   492'-656' | |
|   200m+       656'+ | |
| PAGE CONTINUATION | 12 |
| NATIONAL GRID REFERENCE (Kilometres) | 450 |
| AREAS COVERED BY TOWN PLANS | |

# TOURIST INFORMATION

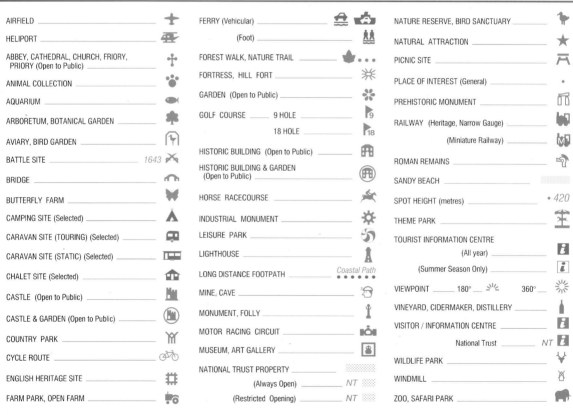

| | |
|---|---|
| AIRFIELD | |
| HELIPORT | |
| ABBEY, CATHEDRAL, CHURCH, FRIORY, PRIORY (Open to Public) | |
| ANIMAL COLLECTION | |
| AQUARIUM | |
| ARBORETUM, BOTANICAL GARDEN | |
| AVIARY, BIRD GARDEN | |
| BATTLE SITE | 1643 |
| BRIDGE | |
| BUTTERFLY FARM | |
| CAMPING SITE (Selected) | |
| CARAVAN SITE (TOURING) (Selected) | |
| CARAVAN SITE (STATIC) (Selected) | |
| CHALET SITE (Selected) | |
| CASTLE (Open to Public) | |
| CASTLE & GARDEN (Open to Public) | |
| COUNTRY PARK | |
| CYCLE ROUTE | |
| ENGLISH HERITAGE SITE | |
| FARM PARK, OPEN FARM | |

| | |
|---|---|
| FERRY (Vehicular) | |
| (Foot) | |
| FOREST WALK, NATURE TRAIL | |
| FORTRESS, HILL FORT | |
| GARDEN (Open to Public) | |
| GOLF COURSE  9 HOLE | |
|              18 HOLE | |
| HISTORIC BUILDING (Open to Public) | |
| HISTORIC BUILDING & GARDEN (Open to Public) | |
| HORSE RACECOURSE | |
| INDUSTRIAL MONUMENT | |
| LEISURE PARK | |
| LIGHTHOUSE | |
| LONG DISTANCE FOOTPATH | Coastal Path |
| MINE, CAVE | |
| MONUMENT, FOLLY | |
| MOTOR RACING CIRCUIT | |
| MUSEUM, ART GALLERY | |
| NATIONAL TRUST PROPERTY | |
| (Always Open) | NT |
| (Restricted Opening) | NT |

| | |
|---|---|
| NATURE RESERVE, BIRD SANCTUARY | |
| NATURAL ATTRACTION | |
| PICNIC SITE | |
| PLACE OF INTEREST (General) | |
| PREHISTORIC MONUMENT | |
| RAILWAY (Heritage, Narrow Gauge) | |
| (Miniature Railway) | |
| ROMAN REMAINS | |
| SANDY BEACH | |
| SPOT HEIGHT (metres) | • 420 |
| THEME PARK | |
| TOURIST INFORMATION CENTRE | |
| (All year) | |
| (Summer Season Only) | |
| VIEWPOINT  180°       360° | |
| VINEYARD, CIDERMAKER, DISTILLERY | |
| VISITOR / INFORMATION CENTRE | |
| National Trust | NT |
| WILDLIFE PARK | |
| WINDMILL | |
| ZOO, SAFARI PARK | |

## SCALE

**1: 42,240**

**1.5 inches to 1 Mile**
**2.4 cm (0.93 inches) to 1 Km**

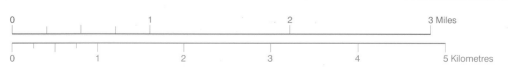

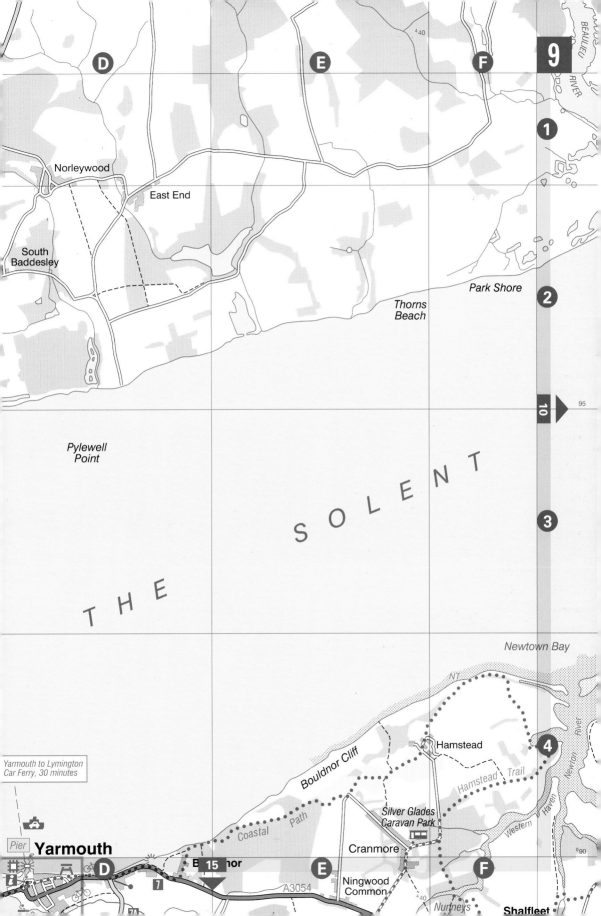

D

E

F

1

Norleywood

East End

South
Baddesley

Park Shore

2

Thorns
Beach

10 ▶ 95

Pylewell
Point

S   O   L   E   N   T

3

Newtown Bay

T   H   E

NT

Bouldnor Cliff

Hamstead

4

Hamstead Trail

Yarmouth to Lymington
Car Ferry, 30 minutes

Coastal   Path

Silver Glades
Caravan Park

Western   Haven

Newton River

0 90

*Pier*   **Yarmouth**

D

B           nor   15   ▼

E

Cranmore

F

7

Ningwood
Common

Shalfleet

A3054

4 40

Nurheys

**A**

**B**

**C**

*BEAULIEU RIVER*

Lepe

Stansore
Point

Stone
Point

**1**

Needs Ore
Point

ark Shore

**2**

**T H E**

**Gur**

*Gurnard Bay*

95

**9**

*Gurnard
Ledge*

*The
Holi*

Rew
Street

*Thorness
Bay*

Sunnycott
Caravan Park

Comfor
Campi

**3**

NT

Burnt
Wood

Thorness Bay
Holiday Park

Great
Thorness

*Newtown Bay*

Mark's
Corner

Little
Whitehouse

*Coastal Path*

**A**

NT

NT

Newtown
Harbour

NT

**Newtown**

*Newton River*

*Clamerkin Lake*

**Porchfield**

*Rodge Brook*

**PARKHU
FORE**

**4**

stead*
Trail*

*Western Haven*

NT

**Locksgreen**

Old
Town Hall

NT

d

90

NT

Corfleath
Firs

Colemans
Animal Farm

**B**

**16**

**C**

45

**7**

**Shalfleet**

ₐ3054

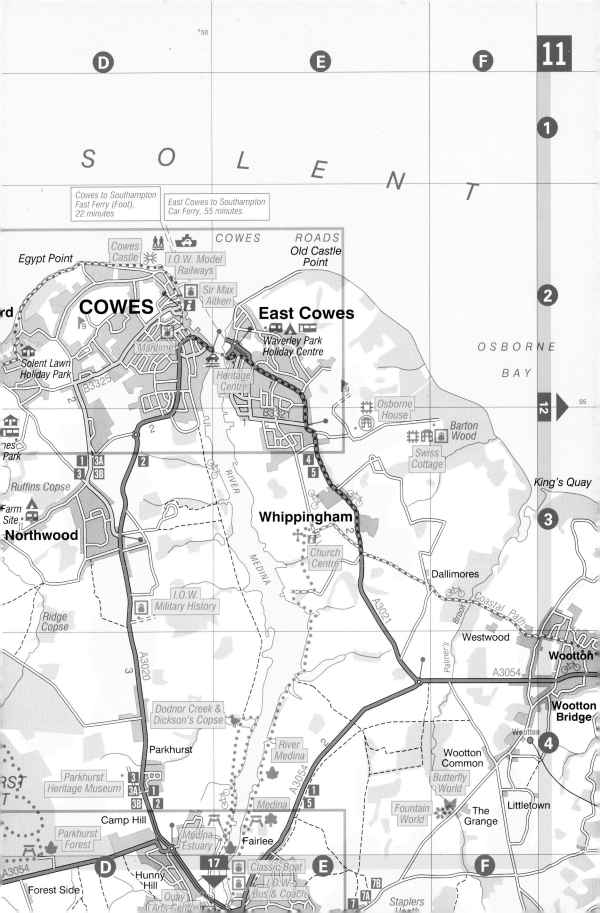

1

S O L E N T

Cowes to Southampton
Fast Ferry (Foot),
22 minutes

East Cowes to Southampton
Car Ferry, 55 minutes

2

COWES ROADS

Old Castle
Point

Cowes
Castle

I.O.W. Model
Railways

Sir Max
Aitken

Egypt Point

**COWES**

**East Cowes**

Waverley Park
Holiday Centre

O S B O R N E

B A Y

Maritime

Solent Lawn
Holiday Park

Heritage
Centre

B3321

Osborne
House

12

95

nes
Park

Barton
Wood

1  3A

Swiss
Cottage

King's Quay

3  3B

2

RIVER

4

3

Ruffins Copse

5

Whippingham

Farm
Site

MEDINA

**Northwood**

Church
Centre

Dallimores

2

A3021

Coastal Path

Brook

I.O.W.
Military History

Ridge
Copse

Westwood

Palmer's

**Wootton**

A3054

**Wootton
Bridge**

Dodnor Creek &
Dickson's Copse

A3020

3

River
Medina

Wootton

4

Parkhurst

Wootton
Common

Butterfly
World

Littletown

Parkhurst
Heritage Museum

3  3A

1

Medina

A3054

1

Fountain
World

The
Grange

3B  2

5

Camp Hill

Medina
Estuary

Fairlee

Parkhurst
Forest

Hunny
Hill

17

Classic Boat

A3054

Forest Side

Quay
Arts Centre

I.O.W.
Bus & Coach

7B

7A

7

Staplers
Heath

90

**Browndown**

**GOSPORT**

*Browndown Point*

A          B          C

1

S t o k e s
B a y

2

T H E

*O S B O R N E*

*B A Y*

S O L E N T

95
◀ 11

*Fishbourne to Portsmouth Car Ferry*

*King's Quay*

3

RYDE    ROADS

Woodside

*Wootton Creek*

Pier    Ryde Pier Head

*Quarr Abbey Church*

*Pier*

**Fishbourne**

*Abbey*

Ryde Esplanade

B3331

Pelhamfield

9

i

Coastal Path

stwood

A3054

1 4 7

**Wootton**

5

7A 7B Quarr Hill

**Binstead**

Ryde St. John's Road

Kite Hill

Weeks    Oakfield

**Wootton Bridge**

*Kite Hill Farm*

Mill Pond

*Firestone Copse*

*Brickfields Horse Country*

Haylands

Swanmore

*Wootton*

4

*Rosemary Vineyard*

**Littletown**

nge

*Blackbridge Brook*

*Havenstreet War Memorial*

Upton

Nunwell Trail

Sma
Ju

A          B          18          C

*Railway*    Havenstreet

Smallbrook Stadium

*Little Upton Farm*

55

*Rowlands Wood*

Deacons

90

Alverstoke

**D**

Clayhill

Old Portsmouth

Southsea

**E**

**PORTSMOUTH**

Eastney

**F**

65

**1**

Gilkicker
Point

※
Spitbank
Fort

**2**

to minutes

Ryde to Portsmouth, Foot Ferry, 15 minutes

Ryde to Southsea, Hovercraft (Foot), 10 minutes

95

※
Horse Sand
Fort

S P I T H E A D

**3**

※
No Man's Land
Fort

**RYDE**

Ryde East
Sands

Appley

Puckpool
Point

Puckpool
Mortar Battery

Harcourt Sands
Holiday Park

Wireless

Tollgate
Holiday Park

Nettlestone
Point

Elmfield

**1**
Puckpool Park

Spring
Vale

**2**
Flamingo
Park

Salterns
Holiday Park

**Seaview**

**4**

**8**

Pondwell

Pondwell
Holiday Park

Seagrove Bay

B3330

Coastal Path

B3340

Horestone
Point

Priory Bay

Waltzing
Waters

NT

**Nettlestone**

9

Node's Point

090

A3055

9

**D**

**19**

**E**

des Point
Holiday Park

※
St. Helen
Fort

**F**

ook
on

field Wood

Field Lane

Hillgrove

B3330

65

⁰90
⁴30

A

B

C

**Keyhaven
(Summer only)**

*Hurst
Castle*

*Model
Railway*

*Sunken
History*

Sconce Point

*Fort Victoria*

Planetarium

*Yarmo
Cast*

Norton

Norton Grange
Classic Resort

Cliff End

Savoy
Holiday Village

1

Colwell Bay

Freshwater

A3054

7A

7

Norton
Green

Brambles Chine

Colwell Bay
Holiday Club

*Golden Hill
Fort*

Warden Point

Colwell

Heathfield Farm
Camping

Beachside
Bungalows

Island Vw.
Chalets

*Golden
Hill*

**Totland**

School Green

*Ivylands
Holiday Park*

**Fres**

A3055

Totland Bay

Pound Green

Middleton

Afton
Marshes

2

NT

Hatherwood
Point

**Headon
Warren**

Stoats Farm
Camping

*Dimbola
Lodge*

**Freshwater
Bay**

B3322

2

7 7A 7B

*Chairlift*

**Tennyson
Down**

Alum Bay

*Marconi*

*Alum Bay
Glass*

**THE
NEEDLES**

*Needles
Old Battery*

*Alum Bay*

*Needles
Park*

NT

Tennyson

Trail

NT

*Tennyson's*

The Nodes

*Tennyson Down
Mortuary Enclosure*

*Tennyson
Down*

*Miniatu
Needle*

Freshwater

*The Needles*

NT

141

NT

*Scratchell's
Bay*

**Main Bench**

85

3

E N G L I S H

4

A

B

C

⁴30

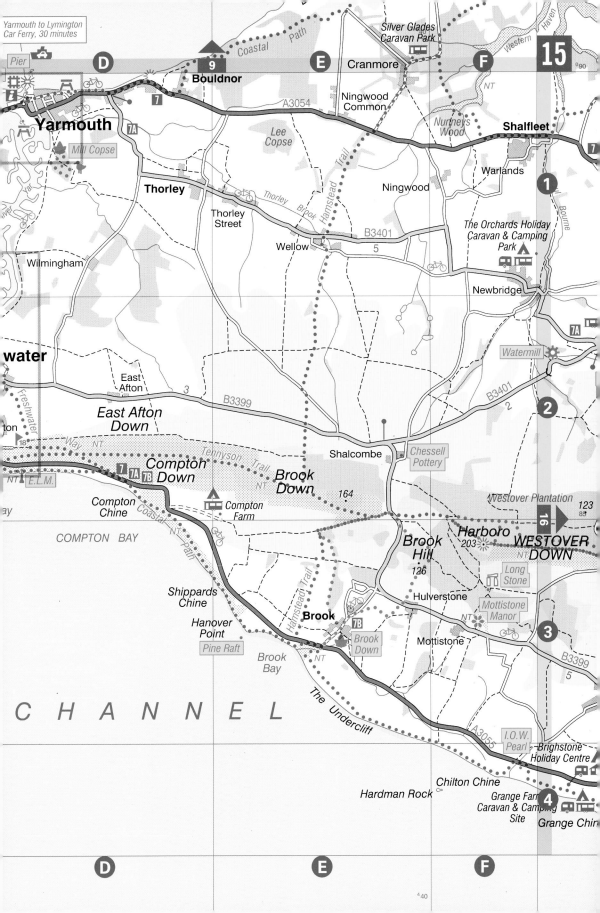

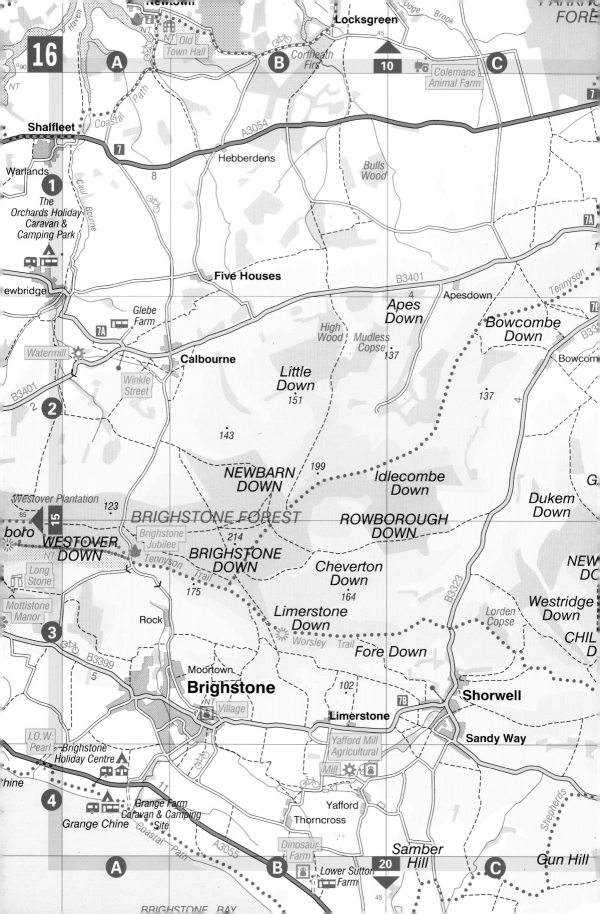

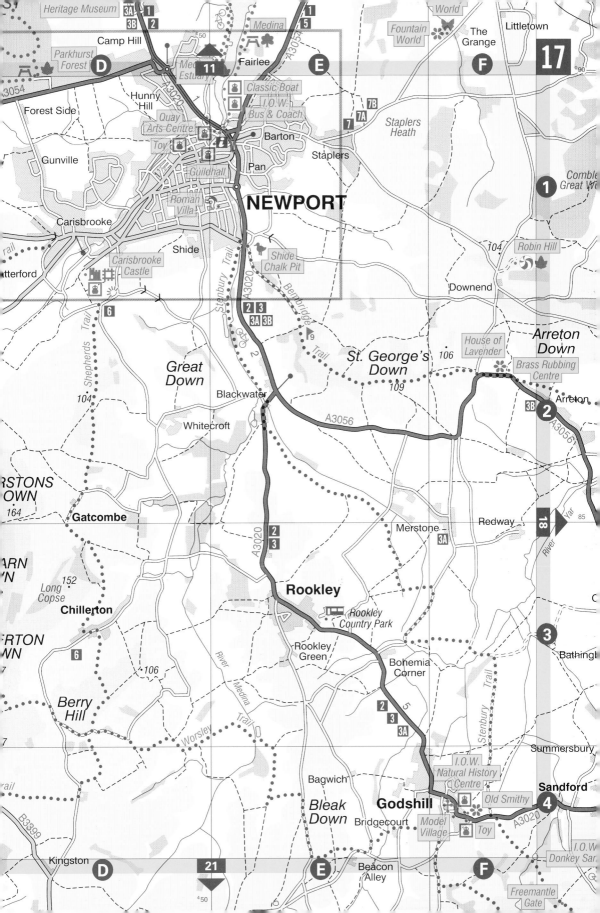

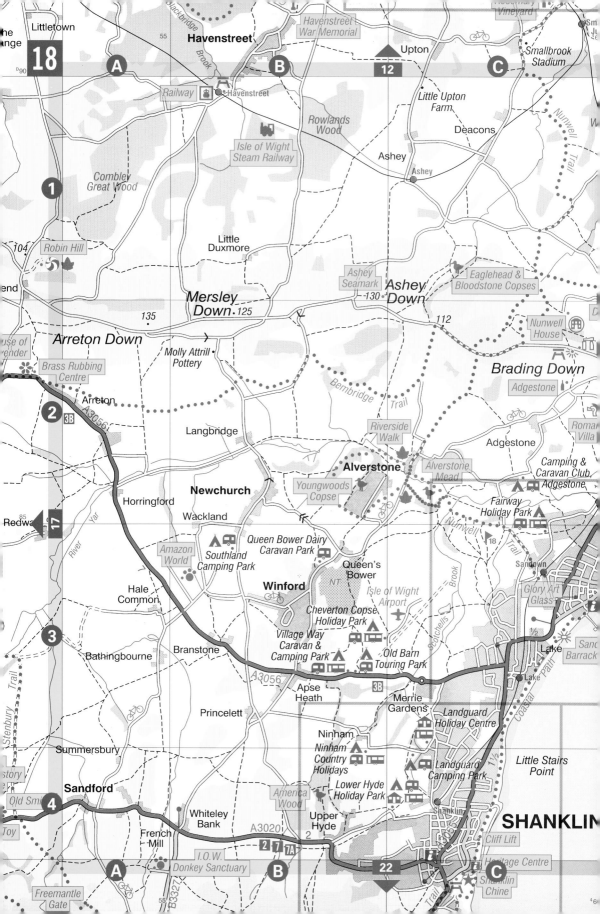

**Nettlestone**    Priory Bay    65

*Waltzing Waters*

~field Wood~

**13**
**1**
**2**

St. Helen's Fort

Nodes Point Holiday Park

Field Lane Holiday Park    Hilgrove Park

**7**
**7A**
**7B**

*Beaper Farm Caravan & Camping Site*

**St. Helens**

*St. Helens*

*Carpenters Farm Camp Site*    1½

Old Mill Holiday Park

Bembridge Point

I.O.W. Shipwreck Centre & Maritime

**Bembridge**

*Lifeboat Station*

Bembridge Harbour

B3330

B3395

B3330

*River Yar*

**1 2**

*Heritage Centre*

Ethel Point

Bembridge Ledge

Lane End

FORELAND

put & Toy    Old Town Hall

3D World

I.O.W. Wax Works

~Devil's~
~~chbowl~

*Bembridge*

NT

*Bembridge*

Bembridge Airport

Coastal Path

*Bembridge Trail*

The Run

Brading

**2**

Hillway

Long Ledge

**Brading**
Yarbridge
B3395

**2**

B3395

Whitecliff Bay Holiday Park

*Morton Manor*    ½

Morton    Yaverland

104    NT

Bembridge Fort    NT

Sandhills Holiday Park

Whitecliff Bay

*Bembridge Down*

**Culver Down**

*Sandown Holidays Chalets*

*I.O.W. Zoo & Sandown Fort*

Sandown Bay Holiday Centre

Yarborough    NT

Culver Battery

B3395

Red Cliff

Whitecliff Ledge

CULVER CLIFF

*Dinosaur Isle*

Fort Spinney Holiday Bungalows

Fort Holiday Park

85

**SANDOWN**

~Pier~
~n~
~ttery~

S A N D O W N

**3**

B A Y

**4**

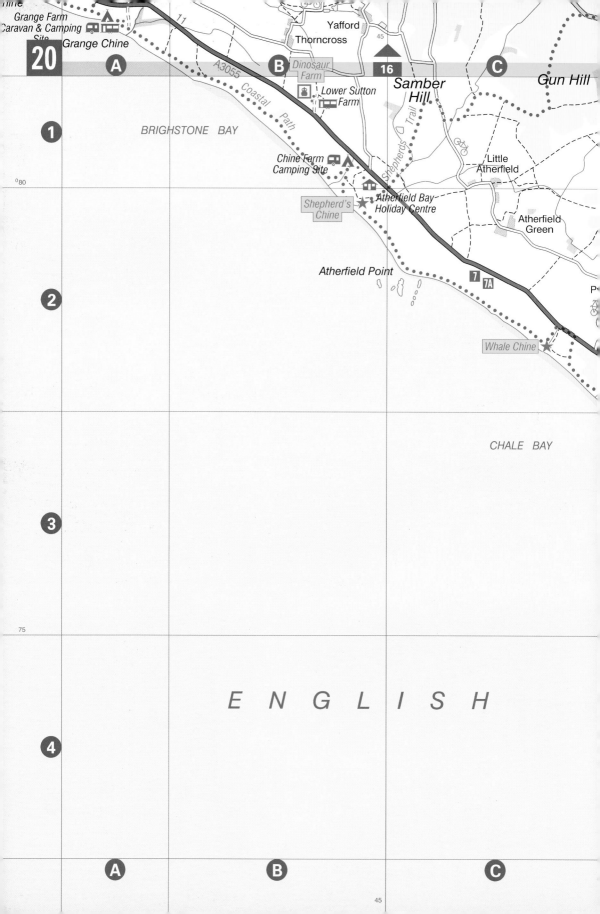

Grange Farm
Caravan & Camping
Site
**Grange Chine**

**A**

Yafford
Thorncross

**B** Dinosaur
Farm

Lower Sutton
Farm

Samber
Hill

16

**C**

Gun Hill

**1**

BRIGHSTONE BAY

Chine Farm
Camping Site

Little
Atherfield

Shepherd's
Chine

Atherfield Bay
Holiday Centre

Atherfield
Green

A3055 Coastal Path

Shepherds Trail

**2**

Atherfield Point

7 7A

Whale Chine

P

CHALE BAY

**3**

75

E N G L I S H

**4**

**A**

**B**

**C**

80

0

45

Bleak
Down

**Godshill**

Bridgecourt

Model
Village

Old Smithy

Toy

Kingston

Donkey Sa

Beacon
Alley

Freemantle
Gate

Ap urcombe
Caravan & Car
Park

Roud

Worsley
Obelisk

**1**

I.O.W.
Owl & Falconry
Centre

Appuldur
House

Chale
Green

Fairfields

•226

STENBURY
DOWN

•209

**2**

Southford

Nettlecombe

Tuttons Hill
Camping

Hoy

**ST. CATHERINE'S
DOWN**

Bierley

WEEK
DOWN

A3055

Kingates

**Whitwell**

**22**

**6**

**Chale**

St. Catherine's
Hill

**Head
Down**

237

Smuggl
Histor

Pelham
Woods

Sawmill

St. Catherine's
Oratory

**St. Lawrence**

St. Catherine's
Quay

Blackgang

Coastal Path

A3055

**7**

Blackgang Chine

Blackgang

**Niton**

The Uncliff

I.O.W.
Rare Bre

**3**

Old
Park

I.O.W.
Glass

Woody
Bay

Rocken End

St. Catherine's

The
Orchard

Undercliff Glen
Caravan Park

Binnel Point

Watershoot
Bay

Castlehaven
Caravan Site

Puckaster Cove

Reeth
Bay

Binnel
Bay

**ST. CATHERINE'S POINT**

75

C H A N N E L

**4**

Sandford

Old Smithy

Toy

Whiteley Bank

French Mill

A3020

America Wood

Upper Hyde

Lower Hyde Holiday Park

**SHANKLIN**

Shanklin

**A**

**2** **B** **7A**

**18**

**C**

Cliff Lift

Heritage Centre

Shanklin Chine

Freemantle Gate

**1**

Appuldurcombe Gardens Caravan & Camping Park

I.O.W. Donkey Sanctuary

Worsley Obelisk

°80

I.O.W. Owl & Falconry Centre

**Wroxall**

Appuldurcombe House

ST. MARTIN'S DOWN

SHANKLIN DOWN

208

235

Worsley

Luccombe Village

*Horse Ledge*

NT

•226

STENBURY DOWN

•209

144

LUCCOMBE DOWN

*Luccombe Bay*

Luccombe Chine

A3055

**7B**

3

**2**

Stenbury Trail

**7**
**7A**

**3**
**3A**

198

WROXALL DOWN

NT 241

NANSEN HILL

•221

*The Landslip*

Lowtherville

NT

St. Boniface Down

Upper Bonchurch

NT

DUNNOSE

WEEK DOWN

**21**

REW DOWN

Rew Down

**6**

Ventnor Heritage

Bonchurch

Monks Bay

Westfield Lodges

Horseshoe Bay

Pelham Woods

Smuggling History

Steephill

Coastal

Ventnor Holiday Villas

**VENTNOR**

**3**

rence

**7** **7A**

A3055

The Undercliff

**2**

Botanic

I.O.W. Rare Breeds

Longshoreman's

Ventnor Bay

Woody Bay

nt

75

*E N G L I S H*

*C H A N N E L*

**4**

**A**

55

**B**

**C**

46

# INDEX TO TOWNS, VILLAGES, HAMLETS & LOCATIONS

Winkle Street, Calbourne

*t* - camping sites, *c* - caravan site (touring),
*s* - caravan site (static), *p* - chalet site.

**Appuldurcombe Gardens Caravan & Camping Park**, Appuldurcombe Road, Wroxall, Ventnor, PO38 3EP, Tel: 01983 852597 -1A 18, *cts*.

**Atherfield Bay Holiday Centre**, Military Road, Chale, Ventnor, PO38 2JD, Tel: 01983 740307 -1B 16, *p*.

**Beachside Bungalows**, Fort Warden Road, Colwell, Totland,Totland Bay, PO39 0DE, Tel: 01983 752511 -see Totland & Freshwater plan -1B, *p*.

**Beaper Farm Caravan & Camping Site**, Beaper Shute, Brading Road, Ryde, PO33 1QJ, Tel: 01983 615210 -1D 15, *cts*.

**Brighstone Holiday Centre**, Military Road, Brighstone, Newport, PO30 4DB, Tel: 01983 740244 -4A 12, *ctp*.

**Camping & Caravanning Club, Adgestone**, Lower Road, Adgestone, Sandown, PO36 0HL, Tel: 01983 403432 / 403989 -see Sandown plan -1B, *ct*.
*Formerly Adgestone Camping Park.*

**Carpenters Farm Camp Site**, Carpenters Farm, Carpenters Road, St Helens, Ryde, PO33 1YL, Tel: 01983 872450 -1D 15, *ct*.

**Castlehaven Caravan Site**, Castlehaven Lane, Niton Undercliff, Ventnor, PO38 2ND, Tel: 01983 730461 -3E 17, *s*.

**Cheverton Copse Holiday Park**, Scotchells Brook Lane, Newport Road, Lake, Sandown, PO36 0JP, Tel: 01983 403161 -3B 14, *cts*.

**Chine Farm Camping Site**, Military Road, Atherfield Bay, Chale, Ventnor, PO38 2JH, Tel: 01983 740228 -1B 16, *ct*.

**Colwell Bay Holiday Club**, Madeira Lane, Colwell, Freshwater, PO40 9SR, Tel: 01983 752403 -see Totland & Freshwater plan -1B, *p*.

**Comforts Farm Camping Site**, Pallance Road, Northwood, Cowes, PO31 8LS, Tel: 01983 293888 -3D 7, *ct*.

**Compton Farm**, Military Road, Brook, Newport, PO30 4HF, Tel: 01983 740215 -2E 11, *ts*.

**Fairway Holiday Park**, The Fairway, Sandown, PO36 9PS Tel: 01983 403462 -see Sandown plan -2C, *cts*.

**Field Lane Holiday Park**, Field Lane, St Helens, Ryde, PO33 1UX, Tel: 01983 872779 -see St Helens plan -1B, *s*.

**Fort Holiday Park**, Avenue Road, Sandown, PO36 8BD, Tel: 01983 402858 -see Sandown plan -2E, *s*.

**Fort Spinney Holiday Bungalows**, Yaverland Road, Sandown, PO36 8QB, Tel: 01983 402360 -2D 15, *p*.

**Glebe Farm**, Calbourne, Newport, PO30 4JL, Tel: 01983 531254 -2A 12, *s*.

**Grange Farm Caravan & Camping Site**, Grange Chine, Military Road, Brighstone Bay, Brighstone, Newport, PO30 4DA, Tel: 01983 740296 -4A 12, *cts*.

**Harcourt Sands Holiday Park**, Puckpool Hill, Spring Vale, Ryde, PO33 1PJ, Tel: 01983 5677321 -4D 9, *sp*.

**Heathfield Farm Camping**, Heathfield Road, Colwell, Freshwater, PO40 9SH, Tel: 01983 756756 -see Totland & Freshwater plan -1C, *ct*.

**Hillgrove Park**, Field Lane, St Helens, Ryde, PO33 1UT, Tel: 01983 872802 -see St Helens plan -1B, *s*.

**Island View Chalets**, Island View Holidays Ltd., Fort Warden Road, Colwell, Totland, Totland Bay, PO39 0DA, Tel: 01983 752712 / 721606 -see Totland & Freshwater plan -1B, *p*. *Also known as Colwell Bay Chalets.*

**Ivylands Holiday Park**, Hurst Point View, Broadway, Totland, Totland Bay, PO39 0AN, Tel: 01983 752480 -see Totland & Freshwater plan -2B, *s*.

**Kite Hill Farm**, Firestone Copse Road, Wootton Bridge, Ryde, PO33 4LE, Tel: 01983 882543 -4B 8, *ct*.

**Landguard Camping Park**, Whitecross Lane, Landguard Manor Road, Shanklin, PO37 7PH, Tel: 01983 867028 -see Shanklin plan -2C, *ct*.

**Landguard Holiday Centre**, Whitecross Lane, Landguard Manor Road, Shanklin, PO37 7PH, Tel: 01983 863100 -see Shanklin plan -1C, *sp*.

**Lower Hyde Holiday Park**, Landguard Road, Shanklin, PO37 7LL, Tel: 01983 866131 -see Shanklin plan -3C, *ctsp*.

**Lower Sutton Farm**, Military Road, Brighstone, Newport, PO30 4PG, Tel: 01983 740401 -1B 16, *s*.

**Ninham Country Holidays**, Ninham Farm, Whitecross Lane, Shanklin, PO37 7PL, Tel: 01983 864243 -see Shanklin plan -2B, *cts*.

**Nodes Point Holiday Park**, Nodes Road, St Helens, Ryde, PO33 1YA, Tel: 01983 872401 -1E 15, *ctsp*.

**Norton Grange Classic Resort**, Halletts Shute, Norton, Yarmouth, PO41 0SD, Tel: 01983 760323 -see Yarmouth plan -1A, *p*.

**Old Barn Touring Park**, Cheverton Farm, Newport Road, Apse Heath, Sandown, PO36 9PJ, Tel: 01983 866414 -3B 14, *ct*. *Formerly Cheverton Farm Camping Park / Camping & Caravanning Club, Sandown.*

**Old Mill Holiday Park**, Mill Road, St Helens, Ryde, PO33 1UE, Tel: 01983 872507 -see St Helens plan -2C, *sp*.

**Orchards Holiday Caravan & Camping Park**, The, Main Road, Newbridge, Yarmouth, PO41 0TS, Tel: 01983 531331 / 531350 -1F 11, *cts*.

**Pines Holiday Park**, The, Cockleton Lane, Gurnard, Cowes, PO31 8QE, Tel: 01983 292395 -see Cowes plan -5A, *sp*. *Formerly Gurnard Pines Holiday Village.*

**Pondwell Holiday Park**, Isle of Wight Self Catering Ltd., Pondwell Hill, Pondwell, Ryde, PO33 1QA, Tel: 01983 612330 -see Seaview plan -2A, *ctp*.

**Queen Bower Dairy Caravan Park**, Queen Bower Dairy, Alverstone Road, Queen's Bower, Sandown, PO36 0NZ, Tel: 01983 403840 -3B 14, *c*.

**Rookley Country Park**, Main Road, Rookley, Ventnor, PO38 3LU, Tel: 01983 752712 / 721606 -3E 13, *s*.

**Salterns Holiday Park**, Isle of Wight Self Catering Ltd., Salterns Office, Saltern's Road, Seaview, PO34 5AQ, Tel: 01983 612330 -see Seaview plan -1A & 2A, *p*.

**Sandhills Holiday Park**, Peacock Hill, Whitecliff Bay, Bembridge, PO35 5QB, Tel: 01983 872277 -2E 15, *s*.

**Sandown Bay Holiday Centre**, Yaverland Road, Yaverland, Sandown, PO36 8QR, Tel: 01983 403402 -2D 15, *p*.

**Sandown Holiday Chalets**, Avenue Road, Sandown, PO36 9AP, Tel: 01983 404025 -see Sandown plan -1E, *p*.

**Savoy Holiday Village**, Halletts Shute, Norton, Yarmouth, PO41 0RJ, Tel: 01983 760355 -see Yarmouth plan -2A, *p*.

**Silver Glades Caravan Park**, Solent Road, Cranmore, Yarmouth, PO41 0XZ, Tel: 01983 760172 -4E 5, *s*.

**Solent Lawn Holiday Park**, Isle of Wight Self Catering Ltd., Shore Road, Gurnard, Cowes, PO31 8LA, Tel: 01983 612330 -see Cowes plan -3A, *p*.

**Southland Camping Park**, Winford Road, Newchurch, Sandown, PO36 0LZ, Tel: 01983 865385 -3B 14, *ct*.

**Stoats Farm Camping**, Stoats Farm, Weston Lane, Totland, Totland Bay, PO39 0HE, Tel: 01983 755258 -see Totland & Freshwater plan -4A, *ct*.

**Sunnycott Caravan Park**, Rew Street, Cowes, PO31 8NN, Tel: 01983 292859 -3C 6, *s*.

**Thorness Bay Holiday Park**, Thorness Bay, Thorness Lane, Great Thorness, Cowes, PO31 8NJ, Tel: 01983 523109 -3B 6, *ctsp*.

**Tollgate Holiday Park**, Isle of Wight Self Catering Ltd., Duver Road, Seaview, PO34 5AJ, Tel: 01983 612330 -see Seaview plan -1A, *p*.

**Tuttons Hill Camping**, Tuttons Hill Cottage, Southdown Lane, Chale, Ventnor, PO38 2LJ, Tel: 01983 551277 -2D 17, *t*.

**Undercliff Glen Caravan Park**, The Undercliffe Drive, St Lawrence, Ventnor, PO38 1XY, Tel: 01983 730261 -3E 17, *s*.

**Ventnor Holiday Villas**, Wheelers Bay Road, Cowlease, Ventnor, PO38 1HR, Tel: 01983 852973 -see Ventnor plan -3D, *sp*.

**Village Way Caravan & Camping Park**, Newport Road, Apse Heath, Sandown, PO36 9PJ, Tel: 01983 863279 -3B 14, *cts*.

**Waverley Park Holiday Centre**, Old Road, East Cowes, PO32 6AW, Tel: 01983 293452 -see Cowes plan -2G, *cts*.

**Westfield Lodges**, Shore Road, Ventnor, PO38 1RH, Tel: 01983 853992 -see Ventnor plan -2E, *p*.

**Whitecliff Bay Holiday Park**, Hillway Road, Hillway, Whitecliff Bay, Bembridge, PO35 5PL, Tel: 01983 872671 -2E 15, *ctsp*.

# TOWN PLANS

## TOWN PLAN PAGES

# REFERENCE

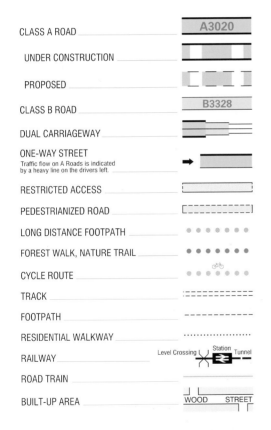

| | |
|---|---|
| CLASS A ROAD | A3020 |
| UNDER CONSTRUCTION | |
| PROPOSED | |
| CLASS B ROAD | B3328 |
| DUAL CARRIAGEWAY | |
| ONE-WAY STREET<br>Traffic flow on A Roads is indicated by a heavy line on the drivers left. | |
| RESTRICTED ACCESS | |
| PEDESTRIANIZED ROAD | |
| LONG DISTANCE FOOTPATH | |
| FOREST WALK, NATURE TRAIL | |
| CYCLE ROUTE | |
| TRACK | |
| FOOTPATH | |
| RESIDENTIAL WALKWAY | |
| RAILWAY | Level Crossing  Station  Tunnel |
| ROAD TRAIN | |
| BUILT-UP AREA | WOOD  STREET |

| | |
|---|---|
| CAR PARK (Selected) | P |
| CHURCH OR CHAPEL | † |
| FIRE STATION | ■ |
| HOSPITAL | H |
| NATIONAL GRID REFERENCE | ⁴60 |
| POLICE STATION | ▲ |
| POST OFFICE | ⊠ |
| TOILET | ▼ |
| EDUCATIONAL ESTABLISHMENT | |
| HOSPITAL OR HOSPICE | |
| INDUSTRIAL BUILDING | |
| LEISURE OR RECREATIONAL FACILITY | |
| PLACE OF INTEREST | |
| PUBLIC BUILDING | |
| SHOPPING CENTRE OR MARKET | |
| OTHER SELECTED BUILDINGS | |

## SCALE

**1:15,840**

4 inches (10.61 cm) to 1 Mile
6.3 cm (2.49 inches) to 1 Km

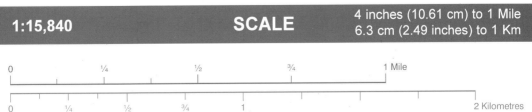

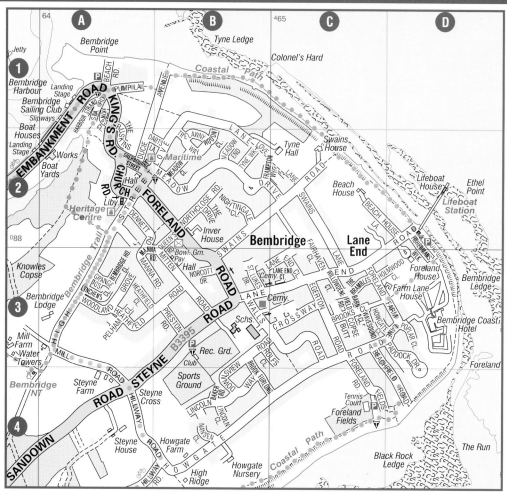

**Bembridge**, situated on the Island's most easterly point (Foreland), is a quiet village, but one of the largest in Europe, situated at the mouth of the shallow Bembridge Harbour. The harbour, a high class yachting centre, is fronted with houseboats and is the home to Bembridge Sailing Club, founded in 1886.

Bembridge was originally a small fishing village virtually cut off from the rest of the Island by Brading Haven, a large expanse of water separating it from St Helens, that stretched from the present harbour two and a half miles to the port of Brading, Yaverland and Sandown. With Bembridge Down to the south-west, the only route to the village was via marshes in Yaverland which flooded in winter, or across the mouth of the harbour which was subject to strong currents at high tide. In 1878, after several only part successful attempts over several centuries, a mile long embankment was built with considerable engineering difficulty from St Helens to the bottom of Kings Road severing the silted up harbour of Brading (q.v.) from the sea and converting the marshland behind into farmland. A short pier was built at this time (subsequently demolished 1928) and with a steamer service and the ease of access provided by the Isle of Wight Railway Company's line from Brading which crossed the embankment in 1882 (closed 1953), Bembridge grew from a tiny fishing village to become a fashionable minor resort.

A peculiarity of Bembridge is the only surviving Post Office model K.1 phonebox in the south of England (on High Street, opposite the junction with Sherbourne Street). This was the first standardised phone box design introduced in 1921.

Bembridge has no seafront and is not well suited for bathing but a long rock ledge (Tyne Ledge, Bembridge Ledge, and Black Rock Ledge), reached from Lane End Road or Foreland Fields Road car parks, runs either side of the lifeboat pier revealing sand and abundant rock pools at low tide ideal for crab hunting.

The Isle of Wight Coastal Path provides a charming walk (4 miles) from Foreland Fields Road car park south-west past Whitecliff Bay with its sandy beach and over Culver Cliff to Yaverland and Sandown.

## PLACES OF INTEREST
◆ BEMBRIDGE HERITAGE CENTRE - 2A. Photographs of Bembridge past & present, memorabilia. Information on Bembridge village, lifeboat & windmill. Rear of Bembridge Library, Church Road
◆ BEMBRIDGE LIFEBOAT STATION - 2D. First established in 1867, a Tyne class lifeboat is now housed at the end of a 76 m (250 ft) long pier built in 1922 to allow launching at all states of the tide. An inflatable 'D' class inshore lifeboat is housed at the foot of the pier. The only other lifeboat on the Island is at Yarmouth. Inshore Lifeboat House, Lane End Road. Tel: 01983 873292.

◆ BEMBRIDGE TOWERMILL - 4A. Four storey hand lufted stone built tower windmill built c.1700 & working until 1913 with a complete set of wooden machinery, much original. The only surviving windmill on the Island where watermills predominated & rare because most tower windmills date from the 19th century. High Street. Tel: 01983 873945.
◆ BEMBRIDGE TRAIL - 1A to 3A. 11 mile (17.5 km) long distance trail running from Newport (Shide Corner, Shide Road, Shide) to Bembridge (Bembridge Point, Embankment Road, Bembridge) via Brading. The east end of the trail joins the Isle of Wight Coastal Path.
◆ ISLE OF WIGHT COASTAL PATH - 2A to 4B. 65 mile (105 km) long distance trail following a circular route around the perimeter of the Island. Except for inland diversions near East Cowes, Newtown & Niton, the coastline is followed as closely as possible. Waymarked by yellow arrows.
◆ ISLE OF WIGHT SHIPWRECK CENTRE & MARITIME MUSEUM (BEMBRIDGE MARITIME MUSEUM) - 2A. Local shipwreck artifacts, antique & modern diving equipment, ship models, audio-visual on diving & lifeboat rescues. Local history & history of the Bembridge lifeboat from 1867. Providence House, Sherbourne Street. Tel: 01983 872223.

## ENTERTAINMENT
◆ Libraries - Church Road.

## SPORT & LEISURE
◆ Bowling Greens - Mitten Road.
◆ Parks & Gardens - Foreland Fields, Foreland Fields Road. Steyne Road Recreation & Sports Ground, Steyne Road.
◆ Tennis Courts - Foreland Fields, Foreland Fields Road.

Bembridge Towermill

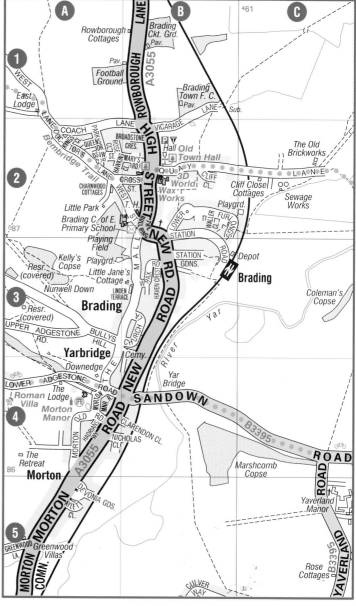

**Brading** is an ancient town dating back to the 13th century when it was granted a Royal Charter. In Roman times Brading Harbour was a busy seaport (exemplified by the siting of Brading Roman Villa), with a quay at the head of the tidal but navigable River Yar forming the western end of Brading Haven, an expanse of water between here and Bembridge (q.v.). The town subsequently developed around the quay and a north-south road which avoided the downs to the west. In medieval times the town's importance as a harbour diminished as the main river channel had become badly silted, becoming too shallow for commercial use, and in the reign of James I the harbour faced competition from Newport Haven on the Medina Estuary which was also had the advantages of the defences of the Cowes forts. The completion (after several attempts between 1562 and 1620) of a successful sea wall across the harbour mouth between St Helens and Bembridge in 1878, finally allowed the reclamation of all the marshes for farmland.

The town has other notable historical connections.

Outside the new town hall of 1902, at the south end of the High Street is the 'Bull Ring', a heavy iron ring fixed into the ground. This is the only visible survival on the Island of the practice of bull-baiting in which a bull, tethered to the ring, would be baited by dogs before being slaughtered. The custom was popular in England in the 16th century and continued until banned by Parliament in the first half of the 19th century.

Little Jane's Cottage, on a footpath off The Mall, was the home of Jane Squibb whose badly weathered gravestone is close by the south-east corner of St Mary's church. She attended Sunday School classes at the church and after her premature death aged 15 in January 1799, was immortalised in 'The Young Cottager' written by the Reverend Legh Richmond, a compassionate Christian, who was Curate in Charge of Brading with Yaverland from 1797 to 1805. Along with 'The Dairyman's Daughter' about Elizabeth Wallbridge of Arreton (who died at age 31 of consumption), it was later included in 'Annals of the Poor', a book of recollections of his experiences in the parish. Published in 1814, it became a best seller in the 19th century running to many millions of copies.

The small enclosure or 'pound' behind the churchyard off Quay Lane was built around 200 years ago to enclose stray animals who could damage growing crops; the offending owner would incur a fine. This lane, which once ran to the quay, continues as the Bembridge Trail footpath crossing the River Yar, and water meadows of the former Brading Haven with its variety of flora and fauna, to Bembridge on a route which passes its windmill. A walk to the west climbing Brading Down (123 m or 403 ft) and Ashey Down is also to be recommended being rewarded with fine views.

## PLACES OF INTEREST

◆ 3D WORLD - 2B. Three dimensional works of art & images in the form of holograms, lenticulars & computer generated 3D graphics. Subjects include portraits, characters & still lifes. Also displays of exceptional 2D artwork. 1 Quay Lane. Tel: 07050 652061.

◆ BEMBRIDGE TRAIL - 1A to 2C. 11 mile (17.5 km) long distance trail running from Newport (Shide Corner, Shide Road, Shide) to Bembridge (Bembridge Point, Embankment Road, Bembridge) via Brading. The east end of the trail joins the Isle of Wight Coastal Path.

◆ BRADING OLD TOWN HALL - 2B. Former town hall restored to present state in 1876 & replaced by the new town hall in 1902. Stocks, whipping post & lock-up in lower market place arcade. Upper room houses a small museum displaying chattels & documents of the town of Brading including the town arms, ancient seal & Act of Parliament, town charter & weights & measures. High Street.

◆ BRADING ROMAN VILLA, THE - 4A. Finest roman villa on the Island discovered in 1880 comprising remains of a large house & farm buildings around courtyard dating from the 4th century. Fine mosaic floors featuring Medusa & a 'cock-headed' man can be found in the undercover west wing. Hypocaust. Exhibition of Roman glass, pottery & finds. Morton Old Road. Tel: 01983 406223.

◆ BRADING ST MARY'S CHURCH - 2B. Not the 'oldest church on the Island', but stands on an early Christian site. Built 1150-1250 & notable for its tower on piers, open on 3 sides- one of only 4 in England. Inside are the De Aula Chapel & the Oglander Chapel in the south aisle with table tombs & memorials to members of the family, amongst the finest on the Island. High Street.

◆ ISLE OF WIGHT WAX WORKS - 2B. Wax works with famous & infamous characters from Island legends & history with sound, light & animation & chamber of horrors. World of Nature with over 100 life-size animal, birds & reptile exhibits set in dioramas, including Professor Copperthwaite's Extraordinary Exhibition of Oddities. 'Where Wax Works' candle carving. Old Rectory Mansion, 46-53 High Street. Tel: 01983 407286.

◆ LILLIPUT ANTIQUE DOLL & TOY MUSEUM, THE - 2B. One of the finest & most comprehensive private collections of old & antique dolls in Britain dating from 2,000 BC to 1945. 2,000 items including dolls houses, teddy bears (c.1904-1935) including some bears made by Steiff, rocking horses, old toys, tin trains, cars & vans. Cornerways, High Street. Tel: 01983 407231.

◆ MORTON MANOR - 4A. Manor dating back to 1249, but rebuilt in 1680, furnished in Georgian period style. Rose & Elizabethan sunken gardens, herbaceous borders, ponds. Traditional Elizabethan turf maze. Possibly the largest London Plane tree in Britain. Japanese acers add colour in autumn. Morton Manor Road. Tel: 01983 406168.

◆ MORTON MANOR VINEYARD - 4A. Vineyard producing mainly white wine, growing grapes suited to the English climate. Estate winery, winegrower's video & small wine making museum in the granary displaying wine-making relics. Morton Manor, Morton Manor Road. Tel: 01983 406168.

## SPORT & LEISURE

◆ Children's Entertainment - Lower Furlongs Playground, Lower Furlongs.
The Mall Playing Field Plaground, The Mall.
◆ Cricket Grounds - Brading Cricket Ground, Rowborough Lane.
◆ Parks & Gardens - The Mall Playing Field, The Mall.

Brading High Street

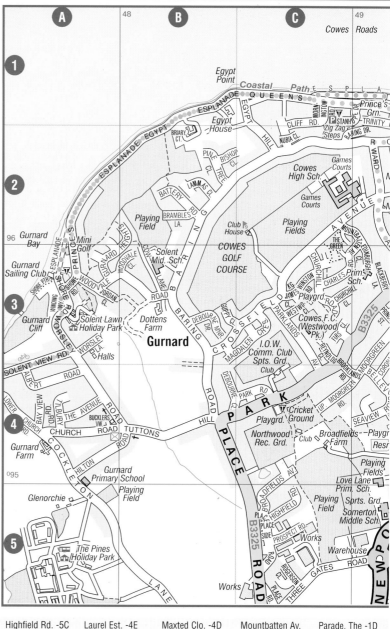

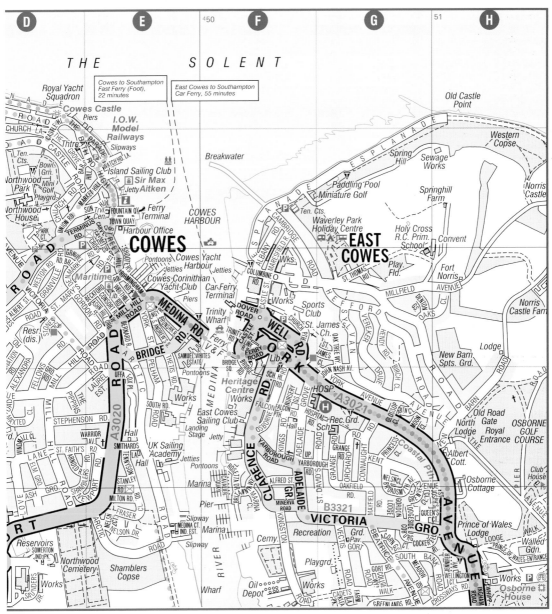

The map shows the area of Cowes and East Cowes on the Isle of Wight, including THE SOLENT, Royal Yacht Squadron, Cowes Castle, I.O.W. Model Railways, COWES HARBOUR, EAST COWES, RIVER MEDINA, Osborne House, and Osborne Golf Course.

Cowes to Southampton Fast Ferry (Foot), 22 minutes

East Cowes to Southampton Car Ferry, 55 minutes

**Cowes** is separated by the River Medina estuary into Cowes (in the west) and East Cowes (in the east), linked by the Cowes Floating Bridge chain ferry. A busy small port, approached by the deep waters of Cowes Roads, with ferry access direct from Southampton, it is the Island's best harbour and the country's main yachting centre.

Cowes grew up around two 'cows' or forts (from which the town received its name), built by Henry VIII on either side of the Medina estuary to guard the harbour entrance. These, together with the others on the Island at Sandown and Yarmouth, and defences on the mainland such as Hurst Castle, were part of the response to the threat of invasion from France. East Cowes Castle (not to be confused with a later mansion by John Nash) was smaller than the fort at (west) Cowes and was abandoned by the end of the 16th century and now no longer exists, whilst part of (west) Cowes Castle still remains (see below).

In the 19th century, the town developed around its shipbuilding industry, the fashionable pastime of yachting (especially after the establishment of the Royal Yacht Squadron and the regular steamer service from Southampton to Cowes in 1820), and the publicity due to the arrival of Queen Victoria at Osborne House. The advent of the Cowes and Newport Railway, later part of the Isle of Wight Central Railway, in 1862 (closed February 1966) also made many parts of the Island accessible from the ferry terminals at Cowes and Ryde. Cowes once had, at different times three piers; the first, Fountain Pier, was built on the current site of the Red Funnel Pontoon in c.1840, the last was demolished in 1962.

Today, (west) Cowes has most of the shopping area attracting tourism and the yachting trade. The winding, narrow and hilly High Street, runs parallel to the shore, extending to Birmingham Road and Medina Road with ship and boat building works. Behind this frontage the 10.5 ha. of Northwood Park, surrounding the council owned Northwood House mansion, offer a quite retreat having many of Cowes recreational facilities. To the north, Prince's Green, fronted by a narrow sand and shingle beach, makes a good viewing point for watching the activities in the Solent, and from here Princes's Esplanade (built 1926) leads westwards to Gurnard Bay (1 mile) with its small sand and shingle beach and limited facilities.

Cowes with its Yacht Harbour is famous for its yachting and boating, being the home of the Royal Yacht Squadron, the world's most famous and exclusive yacht club. Founded as the Yacht Club in 1815, after royal patronage it became the Royal Yacht Club and then the Royal Yacht Squadron in 1833 and moved to Cowes Castle (see below) from The Parade in 1858. Today, the view of the castle, with its red and white striped platform roof, is known throughout the world, the club's start line being the beginning and end of many of the world's greatest yacht and power boat races. Cowes is home to six other major sailing or yacht clubs.

The Island's most important event, Cowes Week is held in the first full week of August. Up to 1,000 yachts race and the week is a sporting and social event of international importance drawing huge crowds. The Round-the-Island Race with nearly 2,000 yachts is held in mid June whilst the Powerboat Weekend is held in September.

On the other side of the estuary, East Cowes (in 1700, just a small village) is one of the quietest towns on the Island and was the only town never to have had a railway station.

Two 'castles' were built in East Cowes at the turn of the 18th century. Norris Castle, a romantic imitation medieval castle, was built in 1799 by architect James Wyatt, for Lord Henry Seymour who entertained many famous guest including Princess Victoria, before she was crowned queen, and the artist Joseph Turner. East Cowes Castle, was a mansion built by John Nash, for himself. The famous Regency architect who designed Regent's Park and Regent Street in London (as well as Newport Guildhall) lived here from 1802. He is buried in St James's Church, a church he designed, on Church Path. The 'castle' was demolished in the 1960s.

Cowes Castle

East Cowes was justly famous for its shipbuilding, centred around Saunders-Roe and J Samuel White, and for the development of the hovercraft. The Saunders-Roe Princess flying boat monoplane built in 1952 was the world's largest and had 10 turbo prop engines. It was intended for the London - New York routes but was superseded by land planes and never entered service. Sir Christopher Cockerell (1910-1999) worked on the design and construction of the world's first man-carrying amphibious hovercraft, the prototype SR.N1, made under contract by Saunders-Roe at East Cowes, during 1958-9, making its first public appearance in June 1959. This was the predecessor of the giant SR.N4 type hovercraft built by the British Hovercraft Corporation at East Cowes, the first of which, the Princess Margaret, inaugurated cross-Channel hovercraft services from Dover as the world's first car-carrying hovercraft on 1st August 1968. The stretched SR.N4 Mk III version of Princess Anne, re-launched at Cowes in April 1978, became the world's largest hovercraft (followed by a similar modification to Princess Margaret in April 1979); both these craft were retired in October 2000. The current GKN Westland Aerospace, the town's major employer, has the world's largest Union Jack (originally painted in 1977, Silver Jubilee Year) on the front of one of its hanger doors; it can be seen from the car ferry.

Today, the Esplanade, with it's grand vista of the yacht activity in Cowes Harbour, and popular sandy beach backed by the recreational facilities on Esplanade Green, should not be missed.

Early Closing- Wednesday.

## PLACES OF INTEREST

Tourist Information Centre (All year) - 2E. 9 The Arcade, Fountain Quay. Tel: 01983 813818 / 291914.
◆ COWES CASTLE - 1D. Henry VIII coastal defence fort built in 1538-9, once one of a pair with East Cowes. Of the original fort only the semi-circular gun platform (with 22 brass signal canons overlooking the Solent) remains. Rebuilt by the architect Salvin, the 'castle' became home to the Royal Yacht Squadron headquarters in 1858. Exterior view only. Royal Yacht Squadron, The Parade.
◆ COWES MARITIME MUSEUM - 3E. Models, painting & photographic archive on the Island's maritime history including naval shipbuilding industry & ship development from sail to steam. RNLI photographs of wrecks & rescues, lifeboat building & launching. Cowes Library, 12-14 Beckford Road. Tel: 01983 293341.
◆ EAST COWES HERITAGE CENTRE - 4F. Exhibition featuring the history, heritage & development of East Cowes over the last 200 years. Temporary local history exhibitions. 8 Clarence Road, East Cowes. Tel: 01983 280310.
◆ ISLE OF WIGHT COASTAL PATH - 4A to 5H. 65 mile (105 km) long distance trail following a circular route around the perimeter of the Island. Except for inland diversions near East Cowes, Newtown & Niton, the coastline is followed as closely as possible. Waymarked by yellow arrows.
◆ ISLE OF WIGHT MODEL RAILWAYS EXHIBITION - 2E. HO scale model railway layout. British Diorama depicting English countryside scenes. American Display depicting Rocky Mountains scene with spectacular high level bridges. Children's layout. Museum housing toy & model trains showing their development from the beginning of the 20th century. Marine Court, The Parade. Tel: 01983 280111.

◆ OSBORNE HOUSE - 5H. Italianate style home of Queen Victoria, built of brick with cement rendering to designs by her husband Prince Albert, the Prince Consort & building contractor Thomas Cubitt between 1845 & 1851. A replacement for an earlier house on this site purchased with the surrounding 138 ha. estate, this was Queen Victoria's seaside retreat which she favoured more than any of her other homes & where she died in 1901. The house has opulent interiors furnished with marbled pillars, statuary & paintings. The Royal Apartments & the Royal Nursery Suite in the Pavilion (the first part of the house finished in 1846 with 32.6 m (107 ft) high flag tower or campanile), part of the Main Wing & part of the servants quarters are open to view as well as the Indian style Durbar Wing (built 1890-91). This contains the Durbar Room, a large ground floor reception room / state banqueting hall with many artifacts from the sub-continent. The Household & Main Wings of the house are not open as they are used as a convalescent home for officers. The terraces outside, graced with a formal Italian garden, give views of the Solent & the surrounding landscaped parkland has a walled garden. Horse & carriage rides connect to Swiss Cottage & Museum half a mile away. Entrance at Prince of Wales Lodge. York Avenue, East Cowes. Tel: 01983 200022.
◆ SIR MAX AITKEN MUSEUM - 2E. Collection of fine maritime paintings, nautical instruments & yachting memorabilia gathered by Sir Max Aitken. Royal Ocean Racing Club, 83 High Street. Tel: 01983 292191.

## ENTERTAINMENT
◆ Bandstands - The Parade.
◆ Libraries - 12-14 Beckford Road, Cowes. 11 York Avenue, East Cowes.
◆ Theatres - Trinity Theatre, The Grove. Tel: 01983 295229.

## SPORT & LEISURE
◆ Bowling Greens - Northwood Park, Ward Avenue.
◆ Children's Entertainment - Brunswick Road Playground, Brunswick Road. Cowes Skateboard Park, Northwood Recreation Ground, Park Road. Esplande Green Paddling Pool, Esplanade, East Cowes. Maxted Close Playground, Maxted Close. Northwood Park Playground, Church Road. Northwood Recreation Ground Playground, Park Road. Vectis Road Playground, Vectis Road, East Cowes. Westwood Close Playground, Westwood Close.
◆ Cricket Grounds - Northwood Cricket Club, Northwood Recreation Ground, Park Road.
◆ Golf Courses - Cowes Golf Course, Crossfield Avenue (2x9 hole). Tel: 01983 280135.
Osborne Golf Course, Osborne House Estate, York Avenue, East Cowes (2x9 hole). Tel: 01983 295421.
◆ Parks & Gardens - Esplanade Green, Esplanade, East Cowes. Jubilee Recreation Ground, York Avenue, East Cowes. New Barn Sports Ground, Old Road, East Cowes. Northwood Park, Ward Avenue. Northwood Recreation Ground, Park Road. Princes's Green, Esplanade. Victoria Grove Recreation Ground, Victoria Grove, East Cowes.
◆ Putting Greens - Esplanade Green, Esplanade, East Cowes. Esplanade, Gurnard. Northwood Park, Ward Avenue.
◆ Tennis Courts - Esplanade Green, Esplanade, East Cowes. Northwood Park, Ward Avenue.

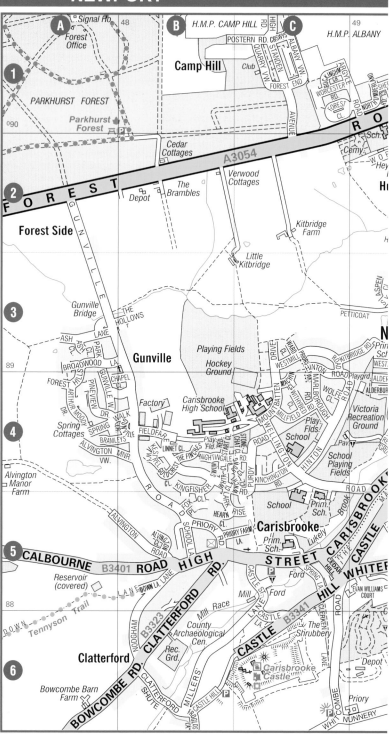

1st 3 Rows    0983 ███    755722    11.35 am

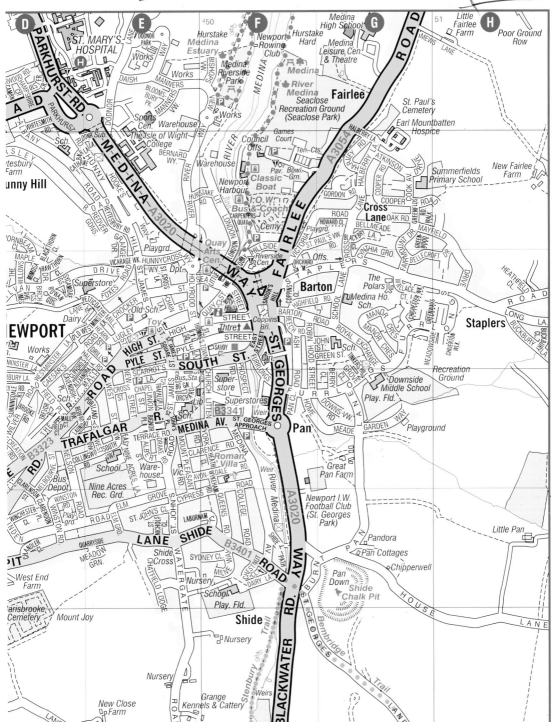

| | | | | | | |
|---|---|---|---|---|---|---|
| Hooke's Way -2E | Hunny Hill -2E | Kitbridge Rd. -3C | Linnet Clo. -4B | Mall Ct. -4D | Manners Vw. -1E | Meadowside -3G |
| Horn Beam Clo. -2D | Hurstake Rd. -2E | Laburnam Clo. -5E | Little London -2F | Mall, The -4D (Carisbrooke Rd.) | Manor Cres. -3G | Medina Av. -4E |
| House La. -5G | John St. -3G | Lark Ri. -5B | Long La. -3H | Mall, The -5C (Cedar Hill) | Maple Dri. -3D | Melbourne St. -4D |
| Howard Clo. -2G | Kestrel Way -4B | Laundry La. -4D | Lugley St. -3E | Malcolm Dyer Ct. -4E (off West St.) | Marlborough Rd. -4C | Mews La. -1G |
| Hunnycross Way -3E | Kinchington Rd. -4C | Limes, The -3D | Machin Clo. -4C | Malthouse Ct. -3E (off Crocker St.) | Mayfield Dri. -2G | Millers' La. -6B |
| | Kingfisher Clo. -4B | Linden Rd. -5D | | | Meadow Grn. -5E | Millfield Rd. -4C |
| | | | | | | Mill St. -3E |

| | | | | | |
|---|---|---|---|---|---|
| Milne Way -5F | Petticoat La. -3C | Robin Hood St. -3F | Savoy Ct. -3F | Tinkers Hill -3G | Wheatear Clo. -4B |
| Mimosa Clo. -3D | Pineview Dri. -4A | Rolla Ct. -4E | Scarrot's La -4E | Towngate Retail Pk. | Whitcombe Rd. -6C |
| Mountbatten Dri. -4C | Portland St. -4E | (off New St.) | School La. -3G | -3E | Whitepit La. -5D |
| Mt. Pleasant Rd. -4E | Postern Rd. -1C | Rowan Gdns. -3D | School La. -5B | (off St James St.) | Whitesmith Rd. -1D |
| Nelson Rd. -4D | Post Office La. -3E | Royal Exchange -3G | Sea St. -3F | Town La. -3F | Willow Ct. -4E |
| New St. -4E | (off High St.) | St Cross Ct. -3E | Sherwood Rd. -1D | Trafalgar La. -4E | (off Laundry La.) |
| Nightingale Rd. -4B | Priors Wlk. -3C | (off Holyrood St.) | Shide Path -5F | Trafalgar Rd. -4D | Willows, The -3D |
| Nine Acres La. -4E | Priory Farm Rd. -5B | St Cross La. -3E | Shide Rd. -5E | Trevor Rd. -4D | Wilver Rd. -4D |
| Nodgham La. -6B | Prospect Rd. -4F | St Georges App. -4F | Snook's Hill -3F | Ulster Cres. -1D | Winchat Clo. -4C |
| Northumberland Rd. | Purdy Rd. -4C | St Georges La. -5F | South St. -3E | Union St. -4E | Winchester Clo. -5D |
| -1D | Pyle St. -3E | St Georges Way -3F | South Vw. -4E | Vicarage Wlk. -3E | Winston Rd. -5D |
| Nunnery La. -6D | Quarryside -5E | St James Sq. -3E | Spring La. -5C | Victoria Rd. -3F | Withybed Clo. -4C |
| Oak Rd. -2G | Quarry Vw. -1C | St James St. -4E | Spring Wlk. -4A | Wallace Ct. -3G | Wolfe Clo. -4C |
| Oakwood Ct. -3D | Quay St. -3F | (St John's Pl.) | Standen Av. -1C | Ward Clo. -3C | Worcester Rd. -1C |
| (off Sylvan Dri.) | Quay, The -3F | St James St. -3E | Staplers Rd. -3F | Watchbell La. -3E | Worsley Rd. -2D |
| Old Westminster La. | Queens Rd. -5F | (Hunnycross Way) | Stonechat Clo. -4C | (off Holyrood St.) | Wykeham Rd. -4F |
| -3D | Recreation Ground | St John's Clo. -5E | Sunningdale Rd. -4D | Watergate Rd. -5E | York Rd. -4F |
| Orchard M. -3F | Rd. -4D | St John's Pl. -4E | Swallow Clo. -4B | Wellington Rd. -4C | |
| Orchard St. -4E | Redstart Clo. -4B | St John's Rd. -5E | Sycamore Gdns. -3D | Westmill Rd. -3C | |
| Pan Clo. -4F | Redver Gdns. -2E | St Nicholas Clo. -5E | Sydney Clo. -5E | Westminster La. -3D | |
| Park Clo. -3A | Redwing Clo. -4C | St Paul's Vw. Rd. -2F | Sylvan Dri. -3D | West St. -4E | |
| Parkhurst Rd. -1D | River Way -2E | St Thomas's Sq. -3E | Terrace Rd. -4E | West Vw. -4E | |

**Newport** is the county town and administrative capital of the Isle of Wight. A major shopping and commercial centre at the geographical heart of the Island (the exact centre is at Shide Corner), all major roads converge on the town.

The first development of the area was at Carisbrooke, beginning with a late Roman fort, followed by the Norman castle on the same site. This was the main administrative centre of the Island until the harbour on the tidal River Medina resulted in the growth of Newport as a trading port; the town, dominated by its markets, developing on a line between the castle and the quay, and the lowest fording point of the river (at the end of Pyle Street near the present Coppins Bridge).

Subject to French raids and burnt down in 1377, a grid like pattern of streets emerged in Georgian times and there is now predominantly Georgian and early Victorian architecture. Although the harbour is no longer the centre of the trade that originally gave Newport its importance, some of its former character has been preserved with narrow alleys, squares and the riverside off The Quay and Little London.

Newport has vivid connections with King Charles I. The Jacobean Old Grammar School in lower St James Street (no. 118, now Newport Youth Centre) dating from 1612, one of the oldest buildings in the town, was Charles I's lodging when he left Carisbrooke Castle (the place of his imprisonment- see below) for the conference with the Parliamentary Commissioners in 1648 over the abortive 'Treaty of Newport', during which occurred his swift removal to Hurst Castle and then to his execution on January 30th 1649 at Whitehall, London.

In the parish church of St Thomas (rebuilt 1854 in the decorated gothic style) in St Thomas's Square is a marble monument by Baron Marochetti, commissioned by Queen Victoria, to Princess Elizabeth, the 15 year old daughter of Charles I who died in 1650 after a short imprisonment at Carisbrooke Castle following the execution of her father. The Victorian interior also has an elaborate carved pulpit and the tomb of Sir Edward Horsey, Captain of the Isle of Wight from 1565-82.

Near the church in St Thomas's Square is God's Providence House (no.12, now a restaurant) built in 1701 on the site of a house which was spared the bubonic plague of 1582-3. Litten Park on Church Litten (with its obelisk to Valentine Gray, a chimney sweep) was chosen for the site of the town's cemetery at the time and many plague victims were buried here.

At the north-east corner of St James Square, a former market square, is a monument to Queen Victoria and a bust of Lord Louis Mountbatten, a former governor of the Island whilst nearby is the Guildhall (see below) on the corner of Quay Street and High Street.

Newport was once the hub of the Island's railway network, but the last line closed to passengers in February 1966.

Shide was the home of Professor John Milne, the 'father' of Seismology. He began the systematic study of seismology in Japan and on his return in 1895 set up an observatory (marked by a plaque on Blackwater Road) in use until his death in 1913; during this time Shide became the world centre for the study of earthquakes.

A walk past the former Carisbrooke watermill, using the raised pavement over the Lukely Brook ford on Castle Street and the view of the castle from Whitcombe Road are recommended, as is the quay area of Newport Harbour which backs onto Seaclose Recreation Ground with its recreational facilities.

Early Closing- Thursday.
Market Days- Council car park, Sea Street, Tuesdays all year.

### PLACES OF INTEREST
Tourist Information Centre (All year)- 3F. The Guildhall, High Street. Tel: 01983 813818 / 823366.
◆ BEMBRIDGE TRAIL - 5F to 6G. 11 mile (17.5 km) long distance trail running from Newport (Shide Corner, Shide Road, Shide) to Bembridge (Bembridge Point, Embankment Road, Bembridge) via Brading. The east end of the trail joins the Isle of Wight Coastal Path.

◆ CARISBROOKE CASTLE - 6C. Norman motte & bailey plan castle with 12th century polygonal shell keep, curtain wall, gatehouse dating from 1335 & Elizabethan internal buildings & surrounding artillery earthworks. The chapel of St Nicholas in Castro, rebuilt in 1904-5 is a reproduction of a chapel which stood here in Charles I time. The castle is famous for its 49 m (161 ft) deep well sunk in 1130 still powered by a donkey driven treadwheel introduced in the 17th century (housed within the Well House of 1587), & for the imprisonment (November 1647 to September 1648) of King Charles I during the English Civil War prior to his execution. Interactive displays in the Old Coach House Exhibition gives information on the castle history. Donkey Centre. Castle Hill, Carisbrooke. Tel: 01983 522107.

◆ CARISBROOKE CASTLE MUSEUM - 6C. Displays on the social history of the Island & local archaeology. Paintings of local scenes. Personal possessions of Charles I, Lord Tennyson memorabilia. Great Hall, Carisbrooke Castle, Castle Hill, Carisbrooke. Tel: 01983 523112.

◆ CLASSIC BOAT MUSEUM, THE - 2F. Undercover collection of small sailing & power boats of historic interest dating back to the 19th century, including the second Bembridge oared lifeboat of 1887 & the first motorised lifeboat of 1922. Engines, equipment & boating memorabilia. Art & photographic displays. Seaclose Wharf, The Quay, Newport Harbour. Tel: 01983 533493.

◆ ISLE OF WIGHT BUS & COACH MUSEUM - 2F. Collection of buses, coaches & a former Ryde Pier Tram covering 80 years of passenger transport on the Island dating back as far as the 1880s. The Quay, Newport Harbour. Tel: 01983 533352.

◆ MEDINA ARBORETUM - 1F. Collection of various specimen trees in small arboretum beside the River Medina estuary. Woodland walk. Seaclose Recreation Ground, Fairlee Road.

◆ MEDINA ESTUARY NATURE TRAIL - 1F. 2.5 mile nature trail (not waymarked) running from Medina Riverside picnic site along the west bank of the River Medina estuary to Dodnor Creek & back along the Cowes-Newport Cycleway. River Way.

◆ NEWPORT GUILDHALL MUSEUM OF ISLAND HISTORY - 3F. Former town hall built by John Nash in 1819. Four displays from pre-history to mans' impact on the Island & Island life using hands-on exhibits, touch-screen computers & a video microscope. Art gallery with 18th & 19th century landscape paintings. High Street. Tel: 01983 823366.

◆ NEWPORT ROMAN VILLA - 4F. Remains of a late Romano-British farmhouse built around 280 AD, discovered in 1926. Hypocaust (underfloor heating system), domestic bath suite, Roman style herb garden. Reconstructed rooms & exhibition of artifacts charting the history of the Roman occupation of the Island. Cypress Road. Tel: 01983 529720 (summer) / 823832 (winter).

◆ PARKHURST FOREST FOREST WALK - 1B. 2 waymarked trails of 2.5 & 1.25 miles through 492 ha. of Forest Commission woodland. Red squirrels, & tree species such as scots pines, corsican pines, japanese larch, norway spruce, sitka spruce, lawson cypress, oak & sweet chestnut can be seen. Parkhurst Forest, Forest Road, Parkhurst.

◆ QUAY ARTS CENTRE - 3F. Two refurbished 18th century brewery warehouses housing an arts centre with changing exhibitions of contemporary art & crafts in Michael West & Rope Store Galleries. Sea Street, Newport Harbour. Tel: 01983 822490 / 528825 (exhibitions).

◆ RIVER MEDINA NATURE TRAIL - 3F. 3.5 mile nature trail (not waymarked) running from The Quay, Newport along the east bank of the River Medina estuary, past Seaclose Recreation Ground & on to Whippingham. The Quay.

◆ SHIDE CHALK PIT NATURE RESERVE - 5G. 5 ha. abandoned chalk quarry sunk into chalk escarpment of Pan Down. Illustrates natural recolonization from bare chalk, through chalk grassland with flowering plants, to tall scrub. Pan Down, Burnt House Lane, Shide.

◆ STENBURY TRAIL - 5F to 6F. 9 mile (15 km) long distance trail running from Newport (Shide Corner, Shide Road, Shide) to Ventnor (Ventnor Botanic Garden, The Undercliff, Undercliff Drive). The south end of the trail joins the Isle of Wight Coastal Path indirectly via short nearby footpaths to the coast.

◆ TENNYSON TRAIL - 5B to 6A. 13 mile (12 km) long distance trail running from Carisbrooke (Nodgham Lane) to Alum Bay beach (Alum Bay New Road, Totland). The west end of the trail from Freshwater Bay to Alum Bay follows the same route as the Isle of Wight Coastal Path.

◆ TIMMY TAYLOR'S TOY BOX - 3E. Toys, models, dolls & games from the 1900s to the 1980s including Wild West railway layout. 33 Lugley Street. Tel: 01983 822960.

## ENTERTAINMENT

◆ Cinemas - Cineworld Multiplex Cinema, Furrlongs, Coppins Bridge. Tel: 01983 537570 / 550800.
Medina Movie Theatre, Medina Theatre, Mountbatten Centre, Fairlee Road (Wednesday evenings only). Tel: 01983 527020.

◆ Libraries - Lord Louis Library, Orchard Street.

◆ Theatres - Anthony Minghella Theatre, Quay Arts Centre, Sea Street, Newport Harbour. Tel: 01983 528825. Apollo Theatre, Pyle Street. Tel: 01983 527267.
Medina Theatre, Mountbatten Centre, Fairlee Road. Tel: 01983 527020.

## SPORT & LEISURE

◆ Bowling Greens - Seaclose Recreation Ground, Fairlee Road.

◆ Children's Entertainment - Garden Way Playground, Garden Way. Hooke's Way Playground, Hooke's Way. Nelson Road Playground, Nelson Road. Seaclose Recreation Ground Playground, Fairlee Road. Seaclose Recreation Ground Skate Park, Fairlee Road. Victoria Recreation Ground Playground, Recreation Ground Road. Victoria Road Playground, Victoria Road.

◆ Golf Courses - Newport Golf Course, St Georges Lane, St George's Down, Shide (S of Newport) (2x9 hole). Tel: 01983 525076.

◆ Parks & Gardens - Clatterford Road Recreation Ground, Clatterford Road. Furrlongs Recreation Ground, Furrlongs. Litten Park, Church Litten. Medina Riverside Park, River Way. Nine Acres Recreation Ground, Elm Grove. Seaclose Recreation Ground (Seaclose Park), Fairlee Road. Victoria Recreation Ground, Recreation Ground Road.

◆ Putting Greens - Seaclose Recreation Ground, Fairlee Road.

◆ Sports & Leisure Centres - Isle of Wight College Sports Centre, Isle of Wight College, Dodnor Lane. Tel: 01983 535211.
Medina Leisure Centre, Fairlee Road. Tel: 01983 523767.

◆ Swimming Pools - Medina Swimming Pool, Medina Leisure Centre, Fairlee Road (indoor). Tel: 01983 523767.

◆ Tennis Courts - Medina Leisure Centre, Fairlee Road. Seaclose Recreation Ground, Fairlee Road. Victoria Recreation Ground, Recreation Ground Road.

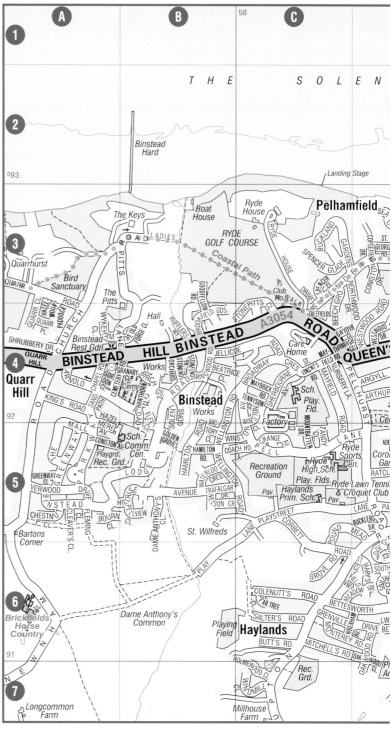

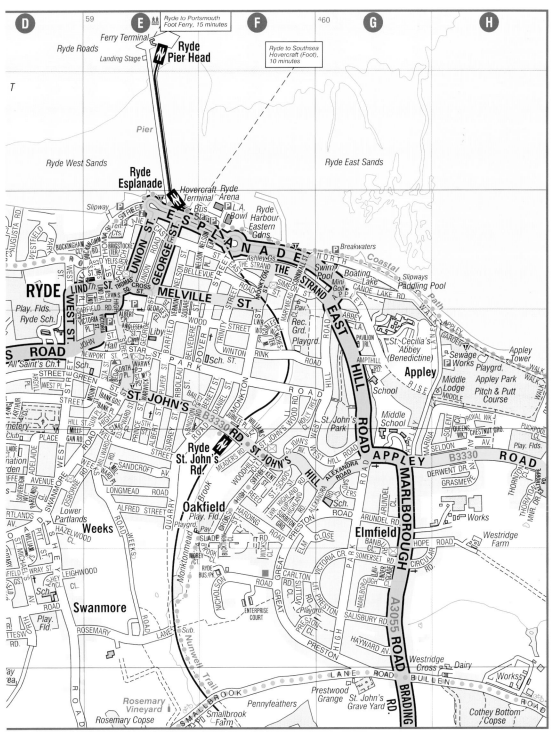

**Ryde** was first developed from two separate communities that were linked in Regency times by Union Street, built in the 1780s. By the 1820s the town had already achieved some status as a fashionable resort. As the principal gateway to the Island it developed earlier than the other Island coastal towns with a pier (see below) and a regular steamer services from Portsmouth by 1825 and this led to the construction of many fine Georgian and Victorian buildings. The opening of the railway line to Shanklin in 1864, however, followed by the Ryde and Newport Railway in 1875, led to a steady decline in the popularity of Ryde in favour of other new railway connected resorts.

Today, Ryde is the Island's largest town and its importance as an arrival and embarkation point continues; Ryde Pier with its ferry terminal at its head, railway stations at either end, and hovercraft terminal and bus station at its foot, is the Island's busiest transport interchange. The town attracts many day-trippers from the mainland.

The visitor to Ryde will first encounter the Esplanade, which continues eastwards (with views to Portsmouth), past Eastern Gardens, with its recreational facilities, and along North Walk, leading along the promenade to the fine Appley Park, and then to Puckpool Park (between Ryde and Seaview, a total of 1.5 miles). Heading uphill, opposite the pier, is Union Street, one of the main shopping streets linking the lower Esplanade area to the hill top above. The Victorian Royal Victoria Arcade (half way up on the right) is of note, as is the Town Hall of 1830 on Lind Street. All Saint's Church (built 1868-72), at the junction of Queen's Road and West Street, designed by Sir George Gilbert Scott, is the most conspicuous of all the churches in Ryde, the tall spire of which (added later), is used as a seamark, whilst the Roman Catholic St Mary's church, on High Street adjacent St Mary's Passage, has a memorial to Lady Hamilton who worshipped here.

Ryde has two gently sloping sandy beaches, Ryde West Sands and Ryde East Sands, either side of the pier. Ryde East Sands fronting the Esplanade and Appley Park, is easily accessible with car parking along North Walk, and at low tide the sand extends for over a mile, although it returns quickly.

Ryde Road Train (dotto train) operates from mid April to the end of October following a route from Puckpool Park (E of Ryde) to Appley Park, Waterside Pool, Esplanade (E end, S of Waterside Boating Lake), Esplanade, George Street, along High Street, Anglesea Street, along George Street, Union Street, Esplanade, Waterside Boating Lake (North Walk side), Appley Park and back to Puckpool Park (E of Ryde).

Early Closing- Thursday.
Market Days- Wednesdays all year.

**PLACES OF INTEREST**

Tourist Information Centre (All year) - 3E. 81-83 Union Street. Tel: 01983 813818 / 562905.
◆ BRICKFIELDS HORSE COUNTRY - 6A. Island's premier equine attraction. Stable yard with shire horses & stallions. Mini World with miniature horses in a miniature world setting. Donkey Town, Farm Corner with milking demonstrations, pigs, rare breeds, waterfowl, fish & poultry. Blacksmiths forge. Museums feature wireless, tractors, racing, carriages, harness, farm heritage & history of the horse. Daily parades in indoor arena, working shire demonstrations, wagon rides, pony rides & pig racing. Newnham Road, Binstead. Tel: 01983 566801 / 615116.
◆ ISLE OF WIGHT COASTAL PATH - 3A to 4H. 65 mile (105 km) long distance trail following a circular route around the perimeter of the Island. Except for inland diversions near East Cowes, Newtown & Niton, the coastline is followed as closely as possible. Waymarked by yellow arrows.
◆ NUNWELL TRAIL - 5F to 7E. 6.5 mile (10.5 km) long distance trail running from Ryde (Ryde St John's Road Station, St John's Road) to Sandown (Sandown Station, Station Avenue).
◆ ROSEMARY VINEYARD - 7E. Island's largest vineyard (12 ha.) planted in 1986. Vineyard trail & working winery with pressing, filtering & bottling processes on view. Smallbrook Lane, Upton. Tel: 01983 811084.

◆ RYDE PIER - 2E. The fourth longest pier, 703 m (2305 ft), in Britain opened in 1814 & used by pedestrians to connect with steamer services to the mainland in the 19th century. A tramway pier (in the middle & now part dismantled) was built in 1864, whilst the railway pier was eventually built in 1880 linking ferries to the Island railway system which previously terminated at Ryde St Johns Road. Esplanade.

## ENTERTAINMENT
◆ Cinemas - Commodore Cinema, 2 Star Street. Tel: 01983 565609.
◆ Concert Venues - Ryde Arena, Quay Road, Esplanade. Tel: 01983 615155.
◆ Libraries - 101 George Street.
◆ Theatres - Ryde Theatre, Lind Street. Tel: 01983 568099.

## SPORT & LEISURE
◆ Boating - Waterside Boating Lake, Esplanade (giant swan pedaloes, canoes).
◆ Bowling Greens - Eastern Gardens, Esplanade. Isle of Wight Indoor Bowls Club, Brading Road (S of Ryde) (indoor). Puckpool Park, Puckpool Hill, Spring Vale (E of Ryde).
◆ Children's Entertainment - Appley Park Play Area, Garden Walk. Coniston Avenue Recreation Ground Playground, Coniston Avenue. Magic Galleon, LA Bowl, The Pavilion, Esplanade (children's indoor adventure play area). Tel: 01983 617070. Preston Close Playground, Preston Close. Puckpool Park Playground, Puckpool Hill, Spring Vale (E of Ryde). Simeon Street Recreation Ground Playground, Rink Road. Slade Road Playing Field Playground, Slade Road. Waterside Boating Lake Paddling Pool, North Walk.
◆ Crazy Golf Courses - Eastern Gardens, Esplanade. Puckpool Park, Puckpool Hill, Spring Vale (E of Ryde).

◆ Golf Courses - Ryde Golf Course, Binstead Road (2x9 hole). Tel: 01983 614809. Westridge Golf Centre, Brading Road (S of Ryde) (2x9 hole). Tel: 01983 613131.
◆ Ice Rinks - Planet Ice, Ryde Arena, Quay Road, Esplanade. Tel: 01983 615155.
◆ Parks & Gardens - Appley Park, Appley Lane. Ashley Gardens, Esplanade / The Strand. Binstead Rest Garden, Binstead Hill. Binstead. Coniston Avenue Recreation Ground, Coniston Avenue, Binstead. Coronation Garden, Ratcliffe Avenue. Eastern Gardens, Esplanade. Playstreet Lane / Pell Lane Recreation Ground, Playstreet Lane. Puckpool Park, Puckpool Hill, Spring Vale (E of Ryde). St John's Park, East Hill Road. Simeon Street Recreation Ground, Simeon Street. Slade Road Playing Field, Slade Road. Upton Road Recreation Ground, Upton Road, Haylands.
◆ Pitch & Putt Courses - Appley Pitch & Putt, Appley Park, Appley Lane.
◆ Putting Greens - Esplanade (E end, S of Waterside Boating Lake).
Puckpool Park, Puckpool Hill, Spring Vale (E of Ryde).
◆ Sports & Leisure Centres - Ryde Sports Centre, Ryde High School, Pell Lane. Tel: 01983 566641. Westridge Squash Courts, Westridge Centre, Brading Road (S of Ryde). Tel: 01983 566243.
◆ Stadiums - Smallbrook Stadium, Ashey Road (S of Ryde) (speedway racing). Tel: 01983 811180.
◆ Swimming Pools - Waterside Pool, Esplanade (retractable roof). Tel: 01983 563656.
◆ Tennis Courts - Puckpool Park, Puckpool Hill, Spring Vale (E of Ryde). Ryde Lawn Tennis & Croquet Club, Playstreet Lane. Ryde Mead Lawn Tennis Club, Church Lane.
◆ Ten Pin Bowling - LA Bowl, The Pavilion, Esplanade. Tel: 01983 617070.

Appley Park, Ryde

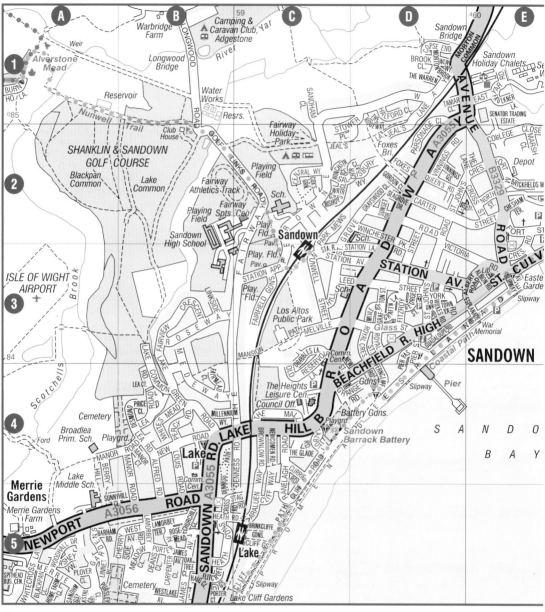

**Sandown** is located on the wide gently curving sweep of Sandown Bay lying between the white Culver Cliff and the dark red promontory of Dunnose. Administratively it is linked with its neighbour Shanklin, and the predominantly residential area of Lake joins both towns. Regarded as the Island's best holiday resort and dominated by hotels and guesthouses, it is frequently recorded as one of the sunniest places on the south coast. The glory of Sandown is its long, gently sloping sandy beach with no rocks or pebbles, a location popular with families and children and, unlike Shanklin, the long Esplanade and Culver Parade are integral with the town behind. The seafront has the usual amusement arcades such as those at the Wight City Leisure Complex and pier (see below) and many recreational facilities off Culver Parade, including Sandham Grounds and Browns Golf. The scenic Ferncliff Gardens and Battery Gardens, west of the pier, offer a quieter environment.

The town grew up in the Victorian era of the mid 19th century from a small village, accelerated by the arrival of the Isle of Wight Railway line from Ryde St John's Road to Shanklin in 1864 and what was to become the Isle of Wight Central Railway, from Newport to Sandown in 1879 (and subsequently closed in 1956). Lewis Carroll stayed at Sandown while collecting material for 'Alice's Adventures in Wonderland'.

Sandown has a notable pre-Victorian history. The long flat beach was the only bay on the southern side of the Island where an invading fleet could land and this military vulnerability led Henry VIII to build a small square plan fort off the coast near Fort Street in the 1540s. Abandoned in the 1580s and subsequently succumbing to the sea, its more sophisticated Charles I replacement of 1632 complete with arrowhead bastions and moat was demolished in 1864 but

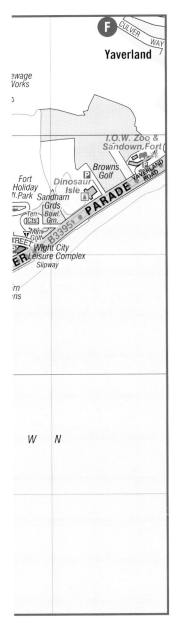

the flat 'v' indented outer shape is still discernible in the layout of Sandham Grounds. The third Palmerston fort at Sandown (see below) is now part of the Isle of Wight Zoo.

Shanklin can be reached by a 2 mile walk south-west along the sea wall revetment or a higher route along the cliff top using the coastal path.

Sandown Road Train (dotto train) operates from mid April to the end of September following a route from Browns Golf to the Isle of Wight Zoo, along Culver Parade, High Street, Esplanade via Pier Street, Esplanade (Eastern Gardens), along Culver Parade, Sandham Grounds (Sandham Gardens) and back to Browns Golf. On Mondays (market day) Fort Street is included.

Early Closing - Wednesday.
Market Days - Wight City Market, Fort Street, Mondays from Easter to end of September. High Street (lower end), Sundays from March to December.

**PLACES OF INTEREST** Tourist Information Centre (All year)- 3D. 8 High Street. Tel: 01983 813818 / 403886.
◆ ALVERSTONE MEAD LOCAL NATURE RESERVE - 1A. Water meadows adjacent to eastern River Yar. Scarce wetland flower species. Dragonflies. Wet willow & alder carr with oak, hazel & cherry on the higher slopes. Alverstone Road / Burnt House Lane, Alverstone.
◆ ALVERSTONE MEAD NATURE TRAIL - 1A. 0.75 mile trail through Alverstone Mead Local Nature Reserve. Starting from Alverstone Road river bridge the trail skirts the southern edge of the reserve, returning on part of the route of the former Isle of Wight Central Railway. Alverstone Mead Local Nature Reserve, Alverstone Road / Burnt House Lane, Alverstone.

◆ DINOSAUR ISLE MUSEUM - 2F. Over 1,000 fossils on display in £2.6 million Pterosaur shaped building using the latest lighting, sound & computer technology. First exhibition area uses fossils to tell the geological story of the Island. The main exhibition hall has dinosaur displays with near complete skeletons & reconstructions. Displays on the Cretaceous period (the Island has the richest early Cretaceous period dinosaur fauna in the world) & Palaeogene period. Due open August 2001. Culver Parade. Tel: 01983 404344.

◆ GLORY ART GLASS - 3D. Hand-blown & sculpted colourful decorative glass including vases & vessels, figurines, flowers, animals, birds, trees, fish & torsos. Twice daily glassmaking demonstrations show the skilled stages involved in the glass production. 22 Melville Street. Tel: 01983 402515.

◆ ISLE OF WIGHT COASTAL PATH - 2F to 5C. 65 mile (105 km) long distance trail following a circular route around the perimeter of the Island. Except for inland diversions near East Cowes, Newtown & Niton, the coastline is followed as closely as possible. Waymarked by yellow arrows.

◆ ISLE OF WIGHT ZOO & JACK CORNEY'S TIGER & BIG CAT SANCTUARY - 2F. Small zoo containing lemurs, monkeys, reptiles, birds, insects & spiders. Big Cat Sanctuary with royal & white bengal tigers, chinese & siberian tigers, leopards, jaguar & black panthers. Yaverland Road, Yaverland. Tel: 01983 403883 / 405562.

◆ NUNWELL TRAIL - 1A to 3C. 6.5 mile (10.5 km) long distance trail running from Ryde (Ryde St John's Road Station, St John's Road) to Sandown (Sandown Station, Station Avenue).

◆ SANDOWN BARRACK BATTERY - 4C. Coastal defence battery built 1861-63. Situated on a 43 m (140 ft) high cliff edge with a ditch on the landward side pierced by a gateway & drawbridge. Formerly armed with 5 guns, the fort is now a municipal garden. Battery Gardens, Talbot Road, Broadway.

◆ SANDOWN FORT - 2F. Small coastal defence battery built 1861-66. Disarmed c.1904 & used for accommodation only, the fort was sold around 1930 & the rear demolished. The remaining sea-facing casemates (some still complete with iron shields) are in use by the Isle of Wight Zoo. Isle of Wight Zoo, Yaverland Road, Yaverland. Tel: 01983 403883 / 405562.

◆ SANDOWN PIER - 4D. 284 m (932 ft) long pier opened c.1879 & extended in 1895. The only entertainment pier left on the Island, the 'new' pavilion was built at the land end in 1934: the one at the seaward end was demolished in the late 1960s. Esplanade. Tel: 01983 404122 / 401754.

## ENTERTAINMENT
◆ Bandstands - Ferncliff Gardens, Ferncliff Road.
◆ Libraries - 119 High Street.

## SPORT & LEISURE
◆ Bowling Greens - Sandham Grounds, Culver Parade.
◆ Children's Entertainment - Battery Gardens Playground, Talbot Road, Broadway. Browns Golf, Culver Parade (children's rides). Tel: 01983 402447. Magic Island, Sandown Pier, Esplanade (children's indoor adventure play area, dodgems, snake slide, children's rides). Tel: 01983 404122 / 401754. Manor Road Playground, Manor Road, Lake. Sandham Rides, Fort Street (giant slide, go-karts, bumper boats). Tel: 01983 406600.
◆ Crazy Golf Courses - Sandham Grounds, Culver Parade. The Lost World Adventure Golf, Sandown Pier, Esplanade.
◆ Golf Courses - Shanklin & Sandown Golf Course, Golf Links Road, The Fairway (18 hole). Tel: 01983 403217.
◆ Parks & Gardens - Battery Gardens, Talbot Road, Broadway. Ferncliff Gardens, Ferncliff Road. Lake Cliff Gardens, Sandown Road, Lake. Los Altos Public Park, Mansion Path. Sandham Grounds (Sandham Gardens), Culver Parade.
◆ Pitch & Putt Courses - Browns Golf, Culver Parade.
◆ Putting Greens - Browns Golf, Culver Parade. Lake Cliff Gardens, Sandown Road, Lake. Sandham Grounds, Culver Parade.
◆ Sports & Leisure Centres - Fairway Sports Centre, Sandown High School, The Fairway. Tel: 01983 406583. The Heights Health & Leisure Base, Broadway. Tel: 01983 405594.
◆ Stadiums - Fairway Athletics Track, Fairway Sports Centre, Sandown High School, The Fairway. Tel: 01983 406583.
◆ Swimming Pools - The Heights Health & Leisure Base, Broadway (indoor). Tel: 01983 405594.
◆ Tennis Courts - Fairway Sports Centre, Sandown High School, The Fairway. Sandham Grounds, Culver Parade.
◆ Ten Pin Bowling - Sandown Pier Superbowl, Sandown Pier, Esplanade. Tel: 01983 404122 / 401754. Wight City Leisure Complex, 37 Culver Parade. Tel: 01983 403658.

Sandown from Battery Gardens

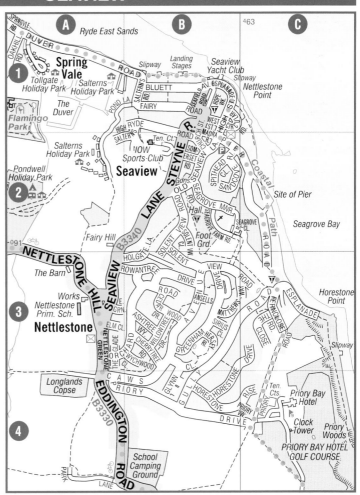

**Seaview** is a small unspoilt seaside village, overlooking Spithead and the Solent, whose principal industry (c.1801) was once the saltpans located in The Duver marshes south of Duver Road. The village is characterised by narrow streets and alleyways, lined with old houses and large Victorian villas. In 1870 a largely unsuccessful attempt was made to develop the village as a resort because of its close proximity to Ryde, and a suspension pier of considerable aesthetic beauty was built midway along Pier Road. Opened in 1881, the pier was 305 m (1,000 ft) long with four suspension towers using wire rope instead of the chain which was more prevalent at the time. It was used by pleasure steamers until WW1 but, despite being the first British pier to be listed, in its dilapidated condition it was destroyed by a gales in December 1950.

Seaview is now a busy sailing centre and Seaview Yacht Club on the Esplanade is one of the premier sailing clubs on the Solent. Most recreational facilities are centred on Puckpool Park immediately to the north-west along the sea wall, whilst sandy beaches can be found at Ryde East Sands, west of Nettlestone Point, and at Seagrove Bay to the east, off Pier Road. Seagrove Bay at its northern end (off the eastern end of the Esplanade or Circular Road) has shingle, and rock pools at low tide.

### PLACES OF INTEREST
◆ FLAMINGO PARK WILDLIFE ENCOUNTER - 1A. Landscaped grounds with over 200 species of birds. Over 100 flamingos, native & foreign ducks, geese, swans, peafowl & cranes. A feature is the feeding of the humboldt penguins, macaws, parrots, giant mirror carp & koi carp. Oakhill Road, Spring Vale. Tel: 01983 612153.

### SPORT & LEISURE
◆ Bowling Greens - Puckpool Park, Puckpool Hill, Spring Vale (NW of Seaview).
◆ Children's Entertainment - Puckpool Park Playground, Puckpool Hill, Spring Vale (NW of Seaview).
◆ Crazy Golf Courses - Puckpool Park, Puckpool Hill, Spring Vale (NW of Seaview).
◆ Golf Courses - Priory Bay Hotel Golf Course, Priory Road (9 hole). Tel: 01983 613146. Westridge Golf Centre, Brading Road, Ryde (W of Seaview) (2x9 hole). Tel: 01983 613131.
◆ Parks & Gardens - Puckpool Park, Puckpool Hill, Spring Vale (NW of Seaview). Sophie Watson Gardens, Steyne Road.
◆ Putting Greens - Puckpool Park, Puckpool Hill, Spring Vale (NW of Seaview).
◆ Sports & Leisure Centres - Isle of Wight Sports Club, Ryde Road. Tel: 01983 613108. Westridge Squash Courts, Westridge Centre, Brading Road, Ryde (W of Seaview). Tel: 01983 566243.
◆ Tennis Courts - Isle of Wight Sports Club, Ryde Road. Tel: 01983 613108. Priory Bay Hotel, Priory Road. Tel: 01983 613146.
◆ Puckpool Park, Puckpool Hill, Spring Vale (NW of Seaview).

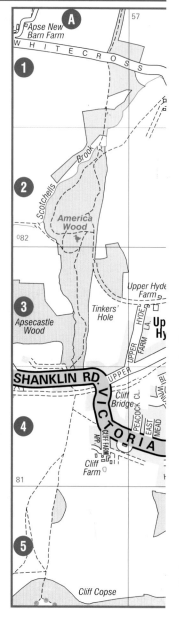

**Shanklin.** One of the best known resorts on the Island, Shanklin is a Victorian inspired town generally regarded as quieter and more refined than Sandown with a slightly less crowded beach and Esplanade. Unlike Sandown, a cliff separates the shops from the gently sloping sandy beach below, reached by using the cliff lift (see below) or the adjacent Osborne Steps. Vehicular access is by the north end of the Esplanade only.

At the south end of the High Street, at the head of Shanklin Chine (see below), is the Old Village made up of a picturesque grouping of thatched cottages, the old Crab Inn (at the junction of Chine Hollow) and Rylstone Gardens, a showpiece garden and lawns, with attractive views and link to the beach reached by Appley Steps. From Luccombe Road a fine walk along the coastal path leads south past

the head of Luccombe Chine and across The Landslip to Bonchurch, whilst northwards a choice of the coastal path or sea wall revetment leads to Sandown.

Keats Green (with its fine hydrangea hedge) is named after the poet John Keats who stayed in Eglantine Cottage (76 High Street, opposite Pomona Road) in 1819 on the second of his two visits to the Island. A plaque marks the spot. Henry Longfellow, the American poet visited Shanklin in July 1868. Above the fountain beside the Crab Inn where he stayed, are some lines written by him.

Shanklin was once graced with a 335 m (1100 ft) long Victorian pier built in 1888, however after becoming semi-derelict by the 1980s, it was destroyed by a storm in 1987. The Island's only surviving railway line, the reason behind the towns development, now terminates at Shanklin.

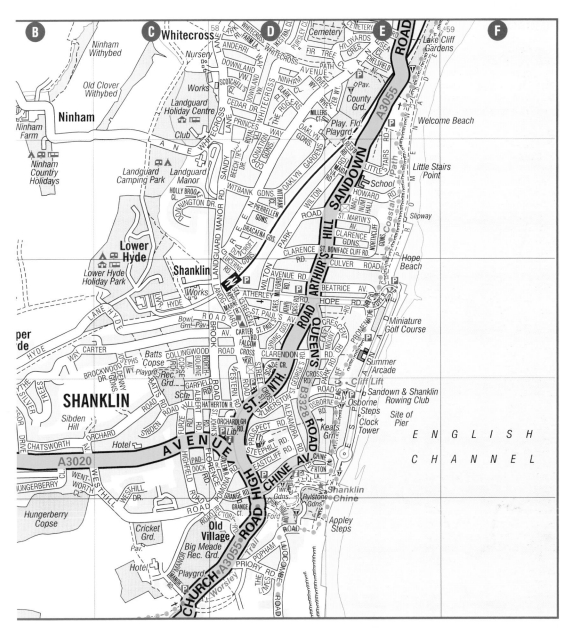

Shanklin Road Train (dotto train) operates from mid April to the end of October following a route from Esplanade (cliff lift) to Esplanade (roundabout at west end), Shanklin Esplanade Golf, Hope Road, Queen's Road, Chine Avenue, along High Street, Regent Street, Atherley Road, along Hope Road, Shanklin Esplanade Golf and back to Esplanade (cliff lift).

Early Closing- Wednesday.

## PLACES OF INTEREST
Tourist Information Centre (All year)- 4D. 67 High Street. Tel: 01983 813818 / 862942.

◆ AMERICA WOOD NATURE RESERVE - 2A. 10.9 ha. deciduous semi-natural ancient woodland. Ancient pasture dominated by mature & pollarded oaks. Information board.

Shanklin Road / Upper Hyde Farm Lane, Upper Hyde.

◆ ISLE OF WIGHT COASTAL PATH - 1E to 5D. 65 mile (105 km) long distance trail following a circular route around the perimeter of the Island. Except for inland diversions near East Cowes, Newtown & Niton, the coastline is followed as closely as possible. Waymarked by yellow arrows.

◆ SHANKLIN CHINE - 4D. Natural scenic wooded sandstone gorge with pathways, bridges & steps running between Chine Hollow in Shanklin Old Village & the Esplanade. Rare ferns. 14 m (45 ft) high waterfall. Opened c.1817. The gorge is Illuminated between mid May & mid September. Chine Hollow / Esplanade. Tel: 01983 866432.

◆ SHANKLIN CHINE HERITAGE CENTRE - 4D. Displays, many pictorial, on the geology & history of Shanklin Chine. Ships, shipwrecks & smuggling, The Victorian Experience, the Chine & WW2 (including a memorial to 40 Royal Marine Commando who trained here) & PLUTO (PipeLine Under The Ocean)- a pipeline laid under the English Channel to supply oil to the Normandy invasion forces in 1944, a section of which is still visible in the gorge. Shanklin Chine, Chine Hollow / Esplanade. Tel: 01983 866432.

◆ SHANKLIN CLIFF LIFT - 4E. Concrete electric vertical lift shaft, approximately 46 m (150 ft) high, built in 1956 connecting Shanklin with the Esplanade (& beach) at the foot of the cliffs thus avoiding a long climb using the adjacent Osborne Steps. The lift has been subject to rebuilds due to continual cliff erosion; the first lift, a Victorian open plan structure, was built here in 1890-92 using a water counter-balance principle, but remained derelict after WW2. Eastcliff Promenade, Palmerston Road / Esplanade. Tel: 01983 862596.

◆ WORSLEY TRAIL - 5C to 5D. 11 mile (18 km) long distance trail running from Shanklin Old Village (High Street, Shanklin) to Brighstone Forest, Brighstone (0.75 miles east of Brighstone Forest car park, Lynch Lane- follow Tennyson Trail). The east end of the trail joins the Isle of Wight Coastal Path indirectly via Chine Avenue or Appley Steps.

## ENTERTAINMENT

◆ Bandstands - Rylstone Gardens, Popham Road.
◆ Libraries - Victoria Avenue.
◆ Theatres - Shanklin Theatre, Steephill Road. Tel: 01983 868000.

## SPORT & LEISURE

◆ Bowling Greens - Brook Road.
◆ Children's Entertainment - Batts Copse Recreation Ground Playground, Batts Road. Big Meade Recreation Ground Playground, Church Road, Shanklin Old Village. County Ground Playing Fields Playground, Oaklyn Gardens. Jungle Jim's, Summer Arcade, Esplanade (children's indoor play area, go-karts). Tel: 01983 867585.
◆ Crazy Golf Courses - Rylstone Gardens, Popham Road. Shanklin Esplanade Golf, Esplanade. The Jungle Adventure Golf, Summer Arcade, Esplanade.
◆ Cricket Grounds - Westhill Road.
◆ Golf Courses - see Sandown.
◆ Parks & Gardens - Appley Green, Chine Hollow. Batts Copse Recreation Ground, Batts Road. Big Meade Recreation Ground, Church Road, Shanklin Old Village. County Ground, Green Lane. Keats Green, Chine Avenue / Osborne Road. Lake Cliff Gardens, Sandown Road. Rylstone Gardens, Popham Road. Tower Gardens, Tower Avenue.
◆ Putting Greens - Rylstone Gardens, Popham Road. Shanklin Esplanade Golf, Esplanade.
◆ Sports & Leisure Centres - see Sandown.
◆ Swimming Pools - Bourne Hall Country Hotel, 11 Luccombe Road (S Shanklin) (indoor). Tel: 01983 862820. Cliff Tops Hotel, 5 Park Road (indoor). Tel: 01983 868558. Hartland Hotel, 41 Victoria Avenue (indoor). Tel: 01983 863123.
◆ Ten Pin Bowling - Summer Arcade, Esplanade. Tel: 01983 867585.

The Old Village, Shanklin

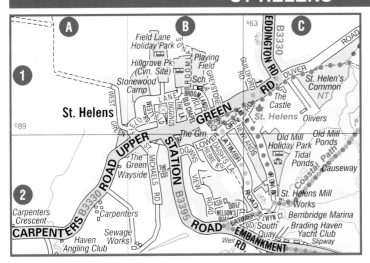

**St Helens** is a small village built around a fine large village green on which cricket is played in the summer. The village, which developed in the vicinity of a 12th century Cluniac priory (now the site of the Priory Bay Hotel, Priory Road - see Seaview plan), lies on high ground adjoining the north-west side of Bembridge Harbour offering good views of its busy marina and the activities at Brading Haven Yacht Club on Embankment Road. A feature of the harbour is the causeway leading from the rebuilt St Helens Mill house to The Duver, once used to impound water in the mill pond behind at high tide, which was released to power the tidemill at low tide.

The Duver, situated to the east of the village along Duver Road, is a spit of land comprising sand dunes colonised with stabilising marram grass abounding with birds and wildlife. Adjoining the National Trust's St Helen's Common, it was formerly a golf links, but was given to the Trust by the Royal Isle of Wight Golf Club in 1961. The beach, especially at the southern tip overlooking the harbour, is sandy and sheltered with shallow water and little tidal flow. On the Promenade are beach huts made from converted grounded railway carriages that once ran on the Island's railways and AP1-88 hovercraft, used on the Southsea to Ryde hovercraft service are manufactured here. At the northern end of the Duver, St Helen's Old Church tower, built from limestone quarried nearby, is now whitewashed

and used as a seamark, most of the churchyard having fallen into the sea in 1550. The rest of the church was subsequently dismantled and a replacement church built in 1717, safely sited inland on Nettlestone Road.

## PLACES OF INTEREST
◆ ISLE OF WIGHT COASTAL PATH - 1C to 2C. 65 mile (105 km) long distance trail following a circular route around the perimeter of the Island. Except for inland diversions near East Cowes, Newtown & Niton, the coastline is followed as closely as possible. Waymarked by yellow arrows.
◆ ST HELENS NATURE TRAIL - 1B. 2 mile nature trail (not waymarked) running from The Green car park, St Helens across St Helen's Common to St Helen's Old Church (now used as a daymark), around the old sandy spit of land known as The Duver (NT), across the old mill pond causeway & back via Mill Road. The Green car park, Upper Green Road.

## SPORT & LEISURE
◆ Children's Entertainment - The Green Playground, Upper Green Road.
◆ Cricket Grounds - The Green, Upper Green Road.
◆ Parks & Gardens - The Green, Upper Green Road.

Seaview

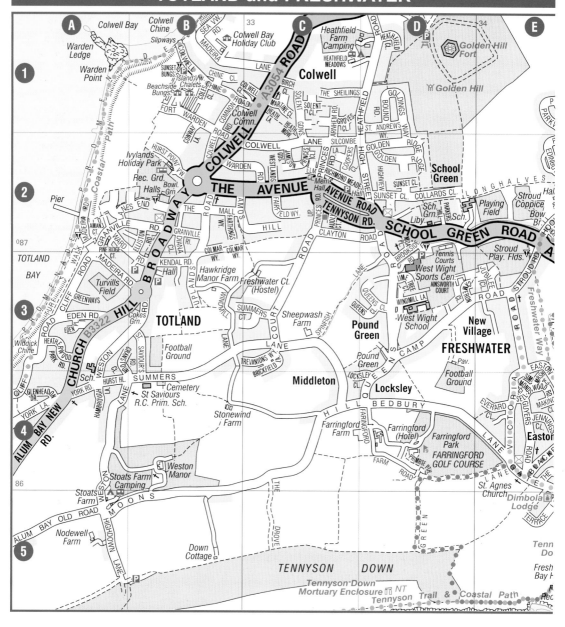

**Totland & Freshwater**. The Freshwater peninsula, almost separated from the rest of the Island by the River Yar, consists of quieter resorts, never as busy as those on the south-east coast. Colwell Bay reached by Colwell Chine Road has a popular long sandy beach with rock pools at low tide offering views to Hurst Castle on the mainland, whilst south of Warden Point, Totland Bay (with its short privately owned pier, built in 1880) has a narrower, less frequented mainly shingle beach with a promenade running down to Widdick Chine.

Freshwater itself is made up of a scattering of smaller villages together forming the largest shopping centre in West Wight. Freshwater Bay has St Agnes church, on Gate Lane, built in 1908 of stone, with a thatched roof, unusual on the Island, and the home of Julia Margaret Cameron

who lived at Dimbola Lodge (see below). The semi-circular bay is a good example of coastal erosion and has a narrow shingle beach backed by a promenade with few facilities.

Freshwater is famous for Farringford, formerly Farringford House and now a hotel, once the home of Alfred Lord Tennyson. Born in Somersby, Lincolnshire in 1809, in 1850 he was appointed the poet laureate, succeeding William Wordsworth after the publication of 'In Memoriam', one of his greatest poems. He rented Farringford in 1853 and then used the proceeds from his poem 'Maud' to buy the property. Attracted by the remote peacefulness of this part of the Island he lived here for nearly 40 years. His presence drew a widening circle of eminent visitors, however the attentions of numerous sightseers became so oppressive that in 1869 he acquired another, quieter house at Aldworth,

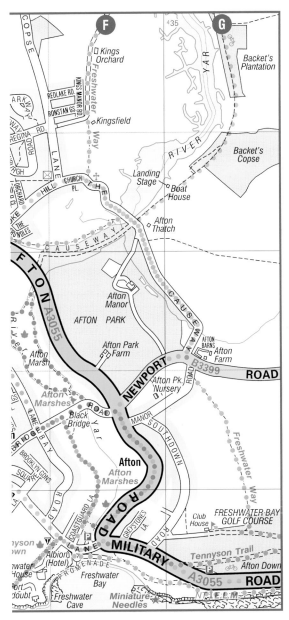

near Haslemere, Surrey where he retreated in the summer, keeping Farringford for the winter months. He died in 1892 and is buried in Westminster Abbey. Tennyson frequently walked the downs (now National Trust), using the back entrance to his property, a bridge over Green Lane. One of the most popular approaches today is to use the Highdown Lane car park or walk along the coastal path.

Early Closing- Freshwater, Thursday. Totland, Wednesday. Market Days- Memorial Hall, Avenue Road, Freshwater, Fridays all year.

## PLACES OF INTEREST

◆ AFTON MARSHES LOCAL NATURE RESERVE - 4F. 15.4 ha. wetland habitat on upper River Yar between Freshwater Bay & Freshwater. Common reed beds, bulrush, clumps of scrub, alder & birch woodland. The River Yar rises at the southern end of the reserve only around 200 m (219 yd) from the sea at Freshwater Bay but flows for 3 miles in the opposite direction to join the Solent at Yarmouth. Afton Road, Freshwater Bay.

◆ AFTON MARSHES NATURE TRAIL - 5F. 2 mile figure of eight trail around Afton Marshes with 11 marked stations. Afton Marshes Local Nature Reserve, Afton Road, Freshwater Bay.

◆ DIMBOLA LODGE - 5E. Former home of pioneer Victorian photographer Julia Margaret Cameron (1815-1879) who photographed many of the famous of Victorian society. Permanent photographic exhibition housing the largest display of her photographs (over 60) in the United Kingdom. Temporary exhibitions, historic cameras, study library. Terrace Lane, Gate Lane, Freshwater Bay. Tel: 01983 756814.

◆ E.L.M. MONUMENT - 5G. Small obelisk on the cliff edge at Afton Down, a memorial to a child with the initials E.L.M. who fell to her death here in 1846. Military Road, Afton Down, Freshwater Bay.

◆ FRESHWATER ALL SAINTS CHURCH - 2F. Late Norman church notable for its memorials to the Tennyson family. Lady Emily Tennyson (Tennyson's wife) is buried in the churchyard. Victorian stained glass. Church Place, Hooke Hill, Freshwater.

◆ FRESHWATER WAY - 1F to 5F & 5G. 4.5 mile (7 km) long distance trail running from Yarmouth (Bridge Road, west of Yarmouth Bridge) to Freshwater (Military Road, Compton, west of the entrance to Compton Farm) or Freshwater Bay (Coastguard Lane, opposite Albion Hotel). All three ends join the Isle of Wight Coastal Path.

◆ GOLDEN HILL COUNTRY PARK - 1D. 20 ha. of woodland surrounding Golden Hill Fort. Colwell Road, Golden Hill, Freshwater.

◆ GOLDEN HILL FORT - 1D. Hexagonal Victorian Palmerston fortified barracks built in 1860 on hill top. Exterior view only. Golden Hill Country Park, Colwell Road, Golden Hill, Freshwater.

◆ ISLE OF WIGHT COASTAL PATH - 1C to 4A & 5D to 5G. 65 mile (105 km) long distance trail following a circular route around the perimeter of the Island. Except for inland diversions near East Cowes, Newtown & Niton, the coastline is followed as closely as possible. Waymarked by yellow arrows.

◆ MINIATURE NEEDLES - 5F. Chalk stacks known as the 'miniature needles'. From west to east- Stag Rock, Arch Rock (once an arch but collapsed in 1992) & Mermaid Rock (which broke from the cliff in 1969). Freshwater Bay.

◆ TENNYSON DOWN MORTUARY ENCLOSURE - 5D. Low rectangular earth bank on slopes of Tennyson Down, the first stage in the construction of a Stone Age long barrow dating from 2500 BC. Tennyson Down, Freshwater Bay.

◆ TENNYSON DOWN NATURE TRAIL - 5F. 2 mile nature trail (not waymarked) running from Freshwater Bay car park, along the west side of Afton Marshes Local Nature Reserve, past St Agnes church, past the rear of Farringford House (& Tennyson's bridge), up to Tennyson Down & back past Fort Redoubt. Freshwater Bay car park, Gate Lane, Freshwater Bay.

◆ TENNYSON TRAIL - 5D to 5G. 13 mile (12 km) long distance trail running from Carisbrooke (Nodgham Lane) to Alum Bay beach (Alum Bay New Road, Totland). The west end of the trail from Freshwater Bay to Alum Bay follows the same route as the Isle of Wight Coastal Path.

## ENTERTAINMENT

◆ Concert Venues - Memorial Hall, Avenue Road, Freshwater.

◆ Libraries - 41 School Green Road, Freshwater.

## SPORT & LEISURE

◆ Bowling Greens - Broadway Recreation Ground, Broadway, Totland.

◆ Golf Courses - Farringford Golf Course, Farringford (Hotel), Bedbury Lane, Freshwater (9 hole). Tel: 01983 752500.
Freshwater Bay Golf Course, Southdown Road, Afton Down, Freshwater Bay (18 hole). Tel: 01983 752955.

◆ Parks & Gardens - Broadway Recreation Ground, Broadway, Totland. Colwell Common, Colwell Common Road, Colwell, Totland. Pound Green, Queens Road, Pound Green, Freshwater. School Green, Parkers Hill, School Green Road, Freshwater. Stroud Playing Fields, School Green Road, Freshwater. Turvills Field, Madeira Road, Totland.

◆ Pitch & Putt Courses - Needles View Pitch & Putt, Headon Hall, Alum Bay New Road, Alum Bay (SW of Totland).

◆ Sports & Leisure Centres - West Wight Sports Centre, Moa Place, Brookside Road, Freshwater. Tel: 01983 752168.

◆ Swimming Pools - West Wight Sports Centre, Moa Place, Brookside Road, Freshwater (indoor). Tel: 01983 752168.

◆ Tennis Courts - West Wight Sports Centre, Moa Place, Brookside Road, Freshwater.

Freshwater Bay

# YARMOUTH

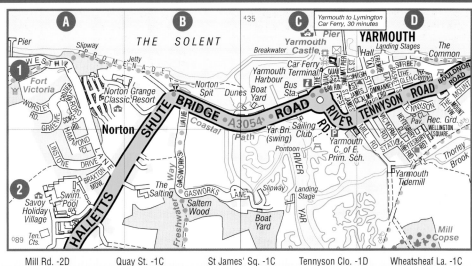

**Yarmouth** is one of the oldest towns on the Island being the first to be granted a Royal Charter in 1135. Situated at the mouth of the western River Yar, the commercial port was once the Island's busiest, however, the town remained compact being restricted by the sea, the low-lying estuarine marshes to the landward side and the River Yar to the west. The river was not bridged until 1863 (the current swing bridge being a modern replacement) and in so doing opened up much of West Wight. Yarmouth was twice sacked and set on fire by the French, in 1377 and 1524, leading to the construction of Yarmouth Castle (see below), a Henry VIII fort, in 1547.

The shortest cross Solent distance is between Yarmouth and the mainland and in 1830 the first steam ship ferry service from Lymington commenced operating a circuitous route via Cowes, Ryde and Portsmouth, the breakwater and creation of the harbour being undertaken later in the mid 1840s. In 1884 the London and South Western Railway extended their line from Lymington to Lymington Pier, beginning a regular connecting steamer service to Yarmouth using the recently constructed pier (see below). In 1889, whilst on the Yarmouth ferry, Alfred Lord Tennyson composed his famous poem 'Crossing the Bar'. Patronage to the town was also increased by the easier access afforded by the Freshwater, Yarmouth and Newport Railway, opened in late 1890 (but closed in 1953). In 1938, the first car ferry to the new ferry terminal, one of the first roll-on-roll-off ferries, began operating and the pier was used less. South Quay and a new breakwater were built in the 1960s and 1970s.

Today's Yarmouth retains its compactness with narrow streets and a picturesque harbour packed, especially in the summer, with moored boats and colourful yachts. Of note are the tiny town hall on Market Square which was built in 1764 and used as a meat market until 1888 and the attractive Yarmouth tidemill off Mill Road. Built in 1793 and now a private house, its waterwheel was powered by the tidal water of Thorley Brook, the main tributary of the Yar. The estuary is a wetland habitat rich in wildlife which may be seen most readily from the town by walking or cycling a short section of the Round-the-Island Cycle Route south from Station Road towards Freshwater. Cruises operate from Yarmouth Pier to view The Needles, to Lymington Town Quay and to Keyhaven where a separate ferry runs to the Henry VIII fort of Hurst Castle.

**PLACES OF INTEREST** Tourist Information Centre (All year) - 1C. The Quay. Tel: 01983 813818 / 760015.

◆ FORT VICTORIA COUNTRY PARK - 1A. Over 20 ha. of coastal woodland (Corsican pines & native deciduous trees) running south-west from Fort Victoria. A feature is the eroding coastline with landslips & dangerous off shore currents. Westhill Lane, Norton. Tel: 01983 760860. See main index for related attractions.

◆ FRESHWATER WAY - 1B to 2B. 4.5 mile (7 km) long distance trail running from Yarmouth (Bridge Road, west of Yarmouth Bridge) to Freshwater (Military Road, Compton, west of the entrance to Compton Farm) or Freshwater Bay (Coastguard Lane, opposite Albion Hotel). All three ends join the Isle of Wight Coastal Path.

◆ MILL COPSE NATURE RESERVE - 2D. 5.6 ha. wood near River Yar. 400 years old until part replanted with conifers by Forestry Commission in the 1960s. Replanted hazel, cherry & oak. Mixed conifers, coastal redwood. Rides. Red squirrels. Freshwater-Yarmouth cycleway, Station Road

◆ MILL COPSE NATURE TRAIL - 2D. Circular ride around central area of Mill Copse Nature Reserve. Bird hide overlooking Barnfields Stream. Mill Copse Nature Reserve, Freshwater-Yarmouth cycleway, Station Road.

◆ YARMOUTH CASTLE - 1C. Henry VIII enclosure fort, completed in 1547, the last addition to his coastal defences. Formerly enclosed by a now infilled moat, the 'castle' has in the south-east corner the first example of an arrowhead bastion to be built in England, an innovation in fort design. Exhibitions of paintings of the Island & photographs of old Yarmouth, local lifeboat crews & lifeboats. Quay Street. Tel: 01983 760678.

◆ YARMOUTH PIER - 1C. 209 m (685 ft) long restored wooden structure opened in 1876, the last surviving wooden pier in Britain. Pier Street.

**SPORT & LEISURE**

◆ Bowling Greens, Crazy Golf Courses, Putting Greens, Tennis Courts - Savoy Holiday Village, Halletts Shute, Norton. Tel: 01983 760355.

◆ Parks & Gardens - Tennyson Close Recreation Ground, Tennyson Close. The Common, Bouldnor Road.

◆ Sports & Leisure Centres, Swimming Pools (indoor & outdoor), Ten Pin Bowling - Savoy Leisure Centre, Savoy Holiday Village, Halletts Shute, Norton. Tel: 01983 760355.

The Esplanade, Ventnor

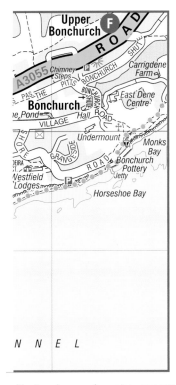

**Ventnor** has a unique story compared to the other towns on the Island. Beginning as a few small farms, watermill and fisherman's hamlet, interest in Ventnor began around 1830 after an article by Sir James Clark, a doctor who had visited the area, extolled the beneficial effects of its mild climate. The promotion of its climate, the result of its south facing position, The Undercliff, and the shelter from northerly winds provided by St Boniface Down, together with the availability of building land and other writers constant reference to the romantic scenery of the coastline, led to the rapid growth in the town's size in the next 20 years. The development, which had no overall planning, was dictated by the hilly terrain and was approaching its growth limits by 1900, however visitors access was now much easier with a pier allowing steam packet ships to dock and the opening of a railway connection, such that by the Edwardian period prior to WW1 the town reached its height as a resort. The climate was the reason behind the building of the Royal National Hospital for Chest Diseases on Undercliff Drive in the late 1860s. Demolished in 1969, the site is now the location of Ventnor Botanic Garden. The Winter Gardens Pavilion was opened in 1936, but in common with many seaside towns, a gentle decline set in from the 1950s. In modern times, being regarded as the warmest spot on the Island, has gained the town the title of the 'English Madeira'.

Ventnor was once graced with a pier and two railway lines.

The first pier was constructed in the early 1860's but was destroyed by the sea, as was its replacement in 1881. The third Royal Victoria pier, opened in 1887, was more long lived being given a major rebuild between 1950 & 1955 but, after requiring expensive repair work in the early 1980s, was sadly demolished in 1993. The site of the pier is now marked by a modern Victorian style bandstand.

The first railway, to Ventnor Town station (now the site of Ventnor Industrial Estate on Old Station Road) was built by the Isle of Wight Railway Company from Ryde St John's Road to Shanklin in 1864 and, despite opposition by the landed gentry, was extended by a tunnel through St Boniface Down to Ventnor in 1866, a route along Luccombe and Bonchurch being rejected. The second, to Ventnor West station (now obscured by Castle Close) was opened by the Isle of Wight Central Railway Company from Merstone via Godshill, and Whitwell to St Lawrence in 1897 and extended via High Hat tunnel eastwards above The Undercliff into Ventnor in 1900. This was the last section of railway to be built on the Island and with its sea views was regarded as one of the most picturesque stretches of railway in Britain. This line closed in 1952, whilst the route from Shanklin closed despite much opposition in April 1966.

Exploring the town today, the visitor will find the centre of the town (of which all the major buildings are Victorian) is laid out in a series of terraces above the sea linked by zig zag roads (one of which bears this name) and some steep flights of steps such as Ninestones Passage between St Boniface Road and Trinity Road and St Alban's Steps linking sections of Gill's Cliff Road. Using these gives a good appreciation of the character of the town. The short Esplanade below is linked at either end to the town above by the steep hairpin bends of Shore Hill, (which runs past the flower gardens of the Cascade on the stream that once powered the watermill), and Bath Road. The Esplanade extends westwards from The Cascade towards Ventnor Park, one of Ventnor's most attractive and popular features, whilst the Eastern Esplanade extends along the sea wall to Monks Bay below Bonchurch. There is a sand and fine shingle beach, which is boulder strewn east of the bandstand.

Ventnor is bordered by the National Trust St Boniface and Bonchurch Downs to the north, part of a designated Area of Outstanding Natural Beauty, whilst the coast from Woody Bay, St Lawrence to Totland Bay is one of the two sections of designated Heritage Coast on the Island (the other is between Bouldnor and Gurnard Ledge, Thorness Bay).

## Bonchurch

The older settlement of Bonchurch is now linked to Ventnor and has many large Victorian villas. Many prominent Victorian literary figures lived in or visited Bonchurch including Charles Dickens in 1849, historian Thomas Macaulay in 1850, children's author Elizabeth Sewell who was much read in the 19th century and the novelist Henry de Vere Stacpoole who wrote 'The Blue Lagoon'. The attractive tree-lined Pond on Bonchurch Village Road, once in his garden, is kept as a memorial to his wife. East Dene was once the childhood home of the poet Algernon Swinburne who is buried in the churchyard of the 'new' St Boniface parish church on Bonchurch Shute.

## The Undercliff

The Undercliff is the result of a 7 mile long geological fault between Blackgang and Luccombe causing landslides that have created a coastal strip of land backed by an inland cliff responsible for much of the mild Ventnor microclimate. The slip occurs at the boundary of unstable greensand (or sandstone) with underlying 'Blue Slipper', a local term for an impervious gault clay, aided by waterlogging caused by the presence of numerous streams. The majority of The Undercliff was created at the time of the last Ice Age, however a major landslide in the early 19th century predated the Victorian development and there have been recurrent slides and falls since, some major (see Blackgang Chine and The Landslip entries). The whole area is rich in plants and vegetation providing a habitat for birds and other wildlife. St Lawrence is the heart of The Undercliff.

Early Closing- Wednesday.
Market Days- High Street car park, Fridays from Easter to December.

## PLACES OF INTEREST

Tourist Information Centre (Summer only)- 2C. 34 High Street. Tel: 01983 813818 / 853625.
◆ BONCHURCH OLD ST BONIFACE CHURCH - 1F. Tiny simple church, mainly medieval but with Norman south door & chancel c.1170, replaced by the new larger parish church inland in 1848. Beautifully set in a tree-sheltered churchyard. Best approached from the east by footpath from The Landslip or from the west by footpath from Shore Road car park. Bonchurch Village Road, Bonchurch.
◆ ISLE OF WIGHT COASTAL PATH - 1F to 3A. 65 mile (105 km) long distance trail following a circular route around the perimeter of the Island. Except for inland diversions near East Cowes, Newtown & Niton, the coastline is followed as closely as possible. Waymarked by yellow arrows.
◆ ISLE OF WIGHT COASTAL VISITORS' CENTRE - 3D Exhibition exploring the animal & plant life of the Island's coastal & marine environment, coastal defence & landslide management. Aquarium with locally caught sea life. Salisbury Gardens, Dudley Road. Tel: 01983 855400.

◆ LONGSHOREMAN'S MUSEUM - 3C. Ventnor's nautical history with a collection of antique engravings & photographs. Models & displays from Victorian times. Esplanade. Tel: 01983 852176.
◆ REW DOWN LOCAL NATURE RESERVE - 2A. 4.6 ha. reserve on steep south facing slope above Ventnor. Chalk grassland flora & fauna. Adonis blue butterflies. Steephill Down Road, Steephill.
◆ ST BONIFACE DOWN 241 m (791 ft) - 1D. Highest point on the Isle of Wight, actually within restricted Ventnor Radar Station site. The road outside the northern perimeter is almost as high, as is much of the surrounding freely accessible National Trust downland offering far reaching views. Ventnor Radar Station, St Boniface Down.
◆ VENTNOR HERITAGE MUSEUM - 2C. History of Ventnor & the villages & coastline of the Undercliff. Notable people associated with Ventnor. Artifacts, old photographs, prints, & models. 11 Spring Hill. Tel: 01983 855407.

## ENTERTAINMENT

◆ Bandstands - Esplanade. Ventnor Park, Park Avenue.
◆ Concert Venues - Winter Gardens, Pier Street. Tel: 01983 855215.
◆ Libraries - High Street.
◆ Theatres - Winter Gardens, Pier Street. Tel: 01983 855215.

## SPORT & LEISURE

◆ Bowling Greens - Mitchell Avenue.
◆ Children's Entertainment - Esplanade Paddling Pool, Eastern Esplanade (Isle of Wight shaped). Havensbush Playground, Old Shute. North Street Playground, North Street. St Margarets Glade Playground, St Margarets Glade. Ventnor Botanic Garden Playground, The Undercliff, Undercliff Drive (W Ventnor). Tel: 01983 855397.
◆ Cricket Grounds - Ventnor Cricket Ground, The Undercliff, Steephill Road (W Ventnor).
◆ Golf Courses - Ventnor Golf Course, Rew Down, Steephill Down Road, Steephill (W Ventnor) (12 hole). Tel: 01983 853326.
◆ Parks & Gardens - Cascade Gardens, Shore Hill. Flowers Brook Recreation Ground, Steephill Road. Salisbury Gardens, Dudley Road. The Pond, Bonchurch Village Road, Bonchurch. Ventnor Park, Park Avenue. Watcombe Bottom Sports Ground, Whitwell Road, Steephill (W Ventnor). Western Cliffs, Bath Road.
◆ Pitch & Putt Courses - Ventnor Towers Hotel, 54 Madeira Road. Tel: 01983 852277.
◆ Putting Greens - St Boniface Road. Ventnor Park, Park Avenue. Western Cliffs, Bath Road.
◆ Sports & Leisure Centres - Rew Valley Sports Centre, Ventnor County Middle School, Newport Road, Lowtherville (organised groups only). Tel: 01983 852884.
◆ Swimming Pools - Ventnor Towers Hotel, 54 Madeira Road (outdoor). Tel: 01983 852277.
◆ Tennis Courts - St Boniface Road. Ventnor Towers Hotel, 54 Madeira Road. Tel: 01983 852277.

# GUIDE TO PLACES OF INTEREST

## HOW TO USE THE PLACE OF INTEREST GUIDE

Places of interest are represented by the appropriate symbol on the map together with red text in a yellow box. The index reference is to the square in which the symbol (or its pointer) appears, not to the box text; e.g. Amazon World -3B 18, is to be found in square 3B on page18.

Entries shown without a main map index reference have the name of the appropriate town plan on which they appear, with an index reference for that plan.
The extent of these town plans are indicated on the main map by a blue box.

Terms such as 'museum', 'country park' etc are omitted from the text on the map.
Entries in italics are not named on the map but are shown with a symbol only.

Entries in italics and enclosed in brackets are not shown on the map.
For both these types of entry the nearest village or town name is given, where that name is not already included in the name of the place of interest.

Places of interest that are open for the summer season only are shown with an **S** symbol after the index reference.

Opening times for places of interest vary considerably depending on the season, day of the week or the ownership of the property. Please check opening times before starting your journey.

**EH**, English Heritage Site.
**NT,** National Trust Property - Always open.
**NT**, National Trust Property - Restricted opening.

---

## Tourist Information Centre

**General information enquiries**, Tel: 01983 813818
*Cowes - see Cowes plan -2E, Tel: 01983* 813818 / *291914.*
*Newport - see Newport plan -3F,*
Tel: 01983 813818 / *823366.*
*Ryde -see Ryde plan -3E, Tel: 01983* 813818 / *562905.*
*Sandown -see Sandown plan -3D,*
Tel: 01983 813818 / *403886.*
*Shanklin -see Shanklin plan -4D,*
Tel: 01983 813818 / *862942.*
*Ventnor -see Ventnor plan -2C,* **S**
Tel: 01983 813818 / *853625.*
*Yarmouth -see Yarmouth plan -1C,*
Tel: 01983 813818 / *760015.*

## Abbey / Friary / Priory

See also Church
**Quarr Abbey -3B 12**. Ruins (precinct walls, a few archways & windows) of a small Cistercian monastery begun in 1131 & dissolved by Henry VIII in 1537 who used much of the stone to build his new coastal forts. Visible only from the adjacent bridleway, which passes through an arch in one of the precinct walls.

## Animal collection

See also Farm Park, Zoo
**Amazon World -3B 18**, Tel: 01983 867122. The story of the Amazon Rainforest. Undercover jungle recreation with over 200 different species of rare & exotic animals, birds, reptiles & insects including snakes, spiders, monkeys & macaws. Outdoor animal enclosures. Adventure play park.
**Brickfields Horse Country** -see Ryde plan -6A.
**Isle of Wight Donkey Sanctuary, The -1A 22**, Tel: 01983 852693. Animal rescue centre established in 1987. Over 200 rescued donkeys & other animals.

## Aquarium

**Fort Victoria Marine Aquarium -1C 14**, **S** Tel: 01983 760283. Locally caught fish & invertebrates including poisonous weever fish, rays, anemones & colour changing cuttlefish. Tropical reef section displays seahorses &

cowfish. Conger Pool.

## Arboretum / Botanical Garden

See also Garden
**Medina Arboretum** -see Newport plan -1F.
**Ventnor Botanic Garden -3A 22**, Tel: 01983 855397. One of the youngest botanic gardens in Britain opened in 1972 on the site of the former Victorian Royal National Chest Hospital (demolished in 1969), but mostly replanted because of frost damage & the storm of October 1987. Thematic plantings along a valley with a warm microclimate that runs east/west parallel to the cliffs include sub tropical, Australasian, palm, culinary & medicinal plants as well as native flora. The Temperate House, opened 1987, displays plants from the southern hemisphere & Oceanic Islands with a photographic display on the former hospital in the foyer. Playground.

## Art Gallery

**Dimbola Lodge** -see Totland & Freshwater plan -5E.
**Quay Arts Centre** -see Newport plan -3F.

## Aviary / Bird Garden

**Flamingo Park Wildlife Encounter** -see Seaview plan -1A, **S**.
**Isle of Wight Owl & Falconry Centre -1A 22**, Tel: 01983 852484 / 840188. Daily flying displays of birds of prey from around the world including vultures. (Indoors in wet weather).

## Butterfly Farm

**Butterfly World -4F 11**, **S** Tel: 01983 883430. 100's of exotic free-flying butterflies from around the world in landscaped tropical indoor garden with ponds, streams, fountains & flowers. Insectarium with jungle nymphs, stick insects, locusts, praying mantis & tarantulas.

## Castle

See also Fortress
**Carisbrooke Castle EH** -see Newport plan -6C.

*Bonchurch Old St Boniface Church* -see Ventnor plan -1F.

*Brading St Mary's Church* -see Brading plan -2B.

*Freshwater All Saints Church* -see Totland & Freshwater plan -2F.

*Godshill All Saints Church* **-4F 17**. Early 14th century church with double nave plan; the fourth church on this site. Unique 15th century 'Christ on the Lily Cross' wall painting & fine monuments. A legend associated with the village tells that the villagers tried three times to build the first Saxon church on level ground to the south, but every night found the stones removed to the current site, hence the name 'God's Hill'.

**Quarr Abbey Church -3B 12**, Tel: 01983 882420. Abbey church of Quarr Abbey, built in 1908-1912 by an order of French Benedictine monks. The church, built of imported rose-red colour Belgian bricks to a design by Dom Paul Bellot, is a notable example of early 20th century construction.

geese & ducks. Children can sit in with the rabbits & feed some of the animals including bottle feeding the lambs. The milking parlour can also be viewed at certain times of year.

**Isle of Wight Rare Breeds & Waterfowl Park -3A 22, S** Tel: 01983 852582 / 855144. One of the largest collections of rare farm animals in the UK. Over 40 species of rare breeds & over 100 species of waterfowl & poultry in 12 ha. coastal park. Temperate waterfall house. Animals include Falabella miniature horses, Sicilian miniature donkeys, African ankole cattle, deer, otters, llamas, meerkats & a guinea pig village.

## Forest Walk / Nature Trail

See also Nature Reserve

**Afton Marshes Nature Trail** -see Totland & Freshwater plan -5F.

**Alverstone Mead Nature Trail** -see Sandown plan -1A.

**Blackgang Nature Trail -3D 21**. 2.5 mile nature trail (not waymarked) running from Blackgang Viewpoint car park, east along Gore Cliff top above the 1928 & 1978 landslips

Yarmouth from the Harbour

*Whippingham St Mildred's Church -3E 11, S Tel: 01983 292130. Victorian gothic & medieval style church designed by Prince Albert & A.J.Humbert with 30.5 m (100 ft) high lantern tower built in 1854-1862. Royal tombs & memorials including one to Prince Albert, Royal Pews & Battenberg Chapel. The Royal Family (including Queen Victoria when at Osborne House) worshiped here.*

## Country Park

**Fort Victoria Country Park** -see Yarmouth plan -1A.

**Golden Hill Country Park** -see Totland & Freshwater plan -1D.

## Farm Park / Open Farm

See also Animal Collection, Zoo

**Colemans Animal Farm -4C 10, S** Tel: 01983 522831. Farmyard with 16th century barn, wooden play area & children's play equipment. Children friendly animals include donkeys, goats, pygmy goats, rabbits, guinea pigs, Shetland ponies, pigs, sheep & lambs. cows, chickens,

(with views of the former Blackgang to Niton road replaced by the current road in 1933) & back via a bridle road.

**Brighstone Forest Jubilee Walk -3A 16**. 3 waymarked trails of 1, 1.75 & 2.5 miles (partly along Tennyson Trail), laid out in 1969 to commemorate the 50th anniversary of the Forestry Commission. Corsican pine, beech, sycamore & copper beech. Green woodpeckers.

**Brook Down Nature Trail -3E 15**. 3.5 mile nature trail (not waymarked) running from Brook Bay car park through Brook to Hulverstone, past Brook Hill House, by the edge of Brook Down (NT), across the head of Compton Valley & returning to Brook again.

**Firestone Copse Forest Walk -4B 12**. 3 waymarked trails of 0.25, 1 & 1.75 miles through 66 ha. of Forest Commission woodland. Broadleaved & conifer trees in pure & mixed stands with rides frequented by nightjars. Herons can be seen on Wootton Mill Pond & in summer butterflies such as white & red admiral, marbled white, small tortoiseshell & fritillary may be observed.

**Fort Victoria Country Park Nature Trail -1C 14**. 1.25 mile waymarked trail with 8 stations through wilderness woodland little affected by man, fern glade & seashore.

**Medina Estuary Nature Trail** -see Newport plan -1F.
**Mill Copse Nature Trail** -see Yarmouth plan -2D.
**Newtown Harbour Nature Trails** NT **-4A 10**. 2 trails of 1 mile & 1.7 miles in length around Newtown Harbour Nature Reserve.
**Parkhurst Forest Forest Walk** -see Newport plan -1B.
**River Medina Nature Trail** -see Newport plan -3F.
**Riverside Walk Nature Trail -2C 18**. 2 mile nature trail (not waymarked) running from a footpath by the side of 'The Mill', Alverstone along south bank of the eastern River Yar (with damp meadows & reedbeds), circling Alverstone Garden Village & back via Alverstone Road.
**Robin Hill Woodland Walks -1F 17**, S. Footpaths, some tarmaced, through woodland including Corsican pine avenue.
**St Helens Nature Trail** -see St Helens plan -1B.
**Tennyson Down Nature Trail** -see Totland & Freshwater plan -5F.

## Fortress

See also Castle
**Bembridge Fort** NT **-2D 19**. Large hexagonal Palmerston fort, built 1862-67 on top of Bembridge Down. In use as industrial units. Exterior view only.
**Cowes Castle** -see Cowes plan -1D.
**Culver Battery** NT **-2E 19**. Coastal defence battery of 1904 on east facing slope of Culver Down. Excavated emplacements.
**Fort Victoria -1C 14**, S Tel: 01983 760860. Palmerston coastal defence battery built 1852-5 to defend the Solent. Part demolished in 1969, the sea-facing casemates remain.
**Golden Hill Fort** -see Totland & Freshwater plan -1D.
**Horse Sand Fort -3F 13**. Palmerston fort built in the 1860s after the Crimean War. Granite & concrete construction. One of the two largest of four built in the Solent. Now derelict. Exterior view only.
**Hurst Castle** EH **-1B 14**, S Tel: 01590 642344. One of the most sophisticated fortresses built by Henry VIII between 1538 & 1543, commanding the narrow entrance to the Solent. Encased in additional fortifications with armoured wings as a Palmerston fort in the 19th century & strengthened again during WW2. Ferry from Yarmouth Pier (via Keyhaven).
**Needles Old Battery, The** NT **-3A 14**, S Tel: 01983 754772. Victorian Palmerston clifftop coastal fort built in 1862 due to threat of French invasion. Exhibition, original gun barrels. 65 m (213 ft) tunnel through cliff giving spectacular view west over The Needles. (Closes in bad weather. 1 mile walk from car park at Alum Bay).
**No Man's Land Fort -3E 13**. Palmerston fort built in the 1860s of granite & concrete construction. One of the two largest of four built in the Solent. There were originally intended to be five forts, however Sturbridge & Ryde Sands were abandoned because of poor foundations being substituted by Spitbank. In use as an adventure activities centre. Exterior view only.
**Puckpool Mortar Battery -4D 13**. Palmerstonian coastal defence mortar battery built 1863-65. Part demolished, the fort is now in a municipal park.
**St Helen's Fort -1E 19**. 1860s Victorian Palmerston (after the prime minister who authorised their construction) fort. One of the two smallest of four built in the Solent. Of granite & concrete construction, one third of the fort (on the seaward side) is clad in layered wrought iron & teak plate armour up to 63 cm (25") thick. Now a private residence. Exterior view only.
**Sandown Barrack Battery** -see Sandown plan -4C.
**Sandown Fort** -see Sandown plan -2F.

**Spitbank Fort -2E 13**, S. Palmerston fort built 1860-1875, one of the two smallest of four built in the Solent. Granite walls, 4.5 m (15 ft) thick at basement level with 63 cm (25") thick wrought iron & teak layered armour on seaward half of fort. 38 ton gun replicas, shell & cartridge hoists. Open to the public. 15 minute boat trip from HM Naval Base, Portsmouth (alongside HMS Warrior).
**Yarmouth Castle** EH -see Yarmouth plan -1C, S.

## Garden

See also Arboretum, Historic Building & Garden
**Fountain World -4F 11**, S Tel: 01983 883430. Display of pools & waterfalls. The formal Italian water garden has computer controlled fountains. The informal Japanese water garden has oriental plants & water features, together with giant ornamental koi carp which are hand fed three times a day.
**House of Lavender -2F 17**, Tel: 01983 528353. Nearly 400 species of herbs & lavenders in 8 themed gardens together with old tools & children's indoor play area.
**Mottistone Manor Gardens** NT **-3F 15**, S Tel: 01983 741302. Colourful herbaceous borders, shrubs & grassy terraces planted with flowering fruit trees laid out in the 1960s & 1970s around an Elizabethan manor house of 1559 (not open). Sea views. Part of the house was buried by a landslide in the early 18th century but subsequently restored.
**Old Smithy, The -4F 17**, S Tel: 01983 840364 / 840889. Landscaped flower garden in the shape of the Island around former blacksmith's forge & cottage. Models of places of interest, grottos, 'Life in the Willows'. Aviaries with tropical birds. Herb garden. Pictorial history of Godshill.

## Historic Building

See also Historic Building & Garden
**Newtown Old Town Hall** NT **-4A 10**, S Tel: 01983 531785. Small town hall c.1699, one of the few remaining buildings of the ancient seaport of Newtown, a classic 'rotten borough' which returned two MPs until 1832. Exhibitions depict ancient Borough documents & exploits of 'Ferguson's Gang'- an anonymous group of Trust benefactors in the 1920s & 1930s.
**Swiss Cottage, Osborne House** EH **-3F 11**, S Tel: 01983 200022. Playhouse for Queen Victoria & Prince Albert's 9 children built 1853-4 containing pantry, kitchen, dining & sitting rooms in grounds of Osborne House. The cottage was built to teach the children the rudiments of housekeeping & cookery. A thatched summerhouse with small size garden implements for the vegetable garden is opposite. Also in the grounds of Osborne House are Victoria Fort, a miniature earth play fort (completed in 1856 after the Crimean war) together with the brick built Albert Barracks of 1860 inside.

## Historic Building & Garden

See also Historic Building, Garden
**Appuldurcombe House** EH **-2A 22**, Tel: 01983 852484 / 840188. Ruined shell of a Palladian mansion (once the grandest on the Island) built by Sir Robert Worsley from 1701, replacing an earlier Tudor manor house. The disused house was badly damaged by a German landmine in 1943 but the east front has been restored. 4.5 ha. of ornamental gardens & 1780s 'Capability' Brown landscaped grounds. Historic Exhibition of prints & photographs depicts the house & its history.
**Morton Manor** -see Brading plan -4A, S.

Osborne House

**Nunwell House -2C 18**, S Tel: 01983 407240. Family home (of the Oglander family) since 1522 with Jacobean & Georgian wings. 2 ha. formal & shrub gardens. Old kitchen exhibition. Family military collection.

**Osborne House EH** -see Cowes plan -5H, S.

## Industrial Monument

See also Windmill

**Calbourne Watermill & Rural Museum -2A 16**, S Tel: 01983 531227. 17th century working (flour) watermill with 6 m (20 ft) diameter overshot waterwheel. 1890s roller-milling plant (rare in a country mill) once used for white flour production. Fire station, wind engine, wildfowl. Rural life exhibits including old agricultural implements & wagons. A 38 ton gun from the former Cliff End Battery, Colwell Bay guards the entrance.

**Yafford Mill -4B 16**, Tel: 01983 740610. Restored 19th century working water mill with overshot wheel last used in 1970 to grind animal feed. Tools & equipment related to millers trade & life on display in mill.

## Leisure Park

See also Theme Park

**Needles Park, The -2B 14**, S Tel: 01983 752401. Children's fun park on cliff top at Alum Bay. Alum Bay sand shop, carousel.

**Robin Hill -1F 17**, S Tel: 01983 527352. 36 ha. of wood & downland with over 20 attractions including 'Colossus' roman galley swinging boat, the Time Machine motion platform cinema, 400 m (437 yd) toboggan run, treetop trail, countryside centre, mazes & Duckdown on the Green child size village.

## Lighthouse

*Hurst Point Lighthouse, Keyhaven -1B 14. 26 m (85 ft) high white round tower built in 1867 guiding vessels through the hazardous western approaches to the Solent. Exterior view only.*

*(Nab Tower, Bembridge -off map area). 27 m (90 ft) high, 12 m (40 ft) diameter cylindrical steel tower on 24 m (80 ft) thick concrete base, flooded & sunk in place in 1920 as a lighthouse replacing the former Nab Light Vessel. Originally designed by G. Menzies as one of a planned line of 8 forts across the English channel joined by steel boom nets to prevent U boat attacks in 1918; on the end of WW1 the only one finished was placed as a lighthouse instead. Exterior view only.*

*Needles Lighthouse, The, Totland -3A 14. Famous red & white banded 31 m (102 ft) high circular granite tower built in 1859 by James Walker (to replace the original on West High Down above). The light, which was automated in 1994, is visible for 14 miles at sea level. Exterior view only.*

**St Catherine's Lighthouse -3D 21**, S Tel: 01983 730284. Battlemented 26 m (85 ft) high white octagonal tower built by James Walker in 1838 at the southernmost tip of the Island. The tower was lowered (from 39 m or 128 ft) in 1875 because the lantern was often shrouded in mist. Third most powerful light in the Trinity House service visible for 26 miles. Automated in 1997. Tours.

**St Catherine's Oratory EH -3D 21**. Octagonal stone west tower (known as the 'Pepper Pot') of oratory used as a medieval lighthouse, built c.1312 by local squire Walter de Godeton. The oratory (now gone) was a small chantry chapel where masses were said for those lost at sea. The lighthouse had a glazed lantern (not an open fire like most medieval lighthouses) but small windows & fog meant the light was of little practical use to shipping. Approached on footpath from Blackgang Viewpoint car park. The stump of another lighthouse, The 'Salt Cellar' (or 'Mustard Pot'), at the base of the radio mast to the south-east, was begun in 1785 but never finished.

## Long Distance Footpath

**Bembridge Trail -1E 17 to 1E 19.** (see Newport, Brading and Bembridge plans).

**Freshwater Way -1C 14 to (2C 14 & 2D 15).** (see Yarmouth and Totland & Freshwater plans).

**Hamstead Trail -3E 15 to 4F 9.** 7 mile (11 km) long distance trail running from Brook (Military Road, Brook Bay) to Newtown Bay (Hamstead Cliffs, 457 m or 500 yd east of Hamstead Ledge, a submerged ridge jutting north-westwards into the sea). The north end of the trail joins the Isle of Wight Coastal Path & the south end does so indirectly via short nearby footpaths to the coast.

Isle of Wight Coastal Path. 65 mile (105 km) long distance trail following a circular route around the perimeter of the Island. Except for inland diversions near East Cowes, Newtown & Niton, the coastline is followed as closely as possible. Waymarked by yellow arrows.

Nunwell Trail -4C 12 to 3C 18. (see Ryde and Sandown plans).

Shepherds Trail -2D 17 to 2B 20. 7.5 mile (12 km) long distance trail running from Carisbrooke (Whitcombe Cross, Whitcombe Road, 183 m or 200 yd west of Carisbrooke Castle Viewpoint at Nunnery car park) to Shepherd's Chine (Military Road, nr. Atherfield). The south end of the trail joins the Isle of Wight Coastal Path.

Stenbury Trail -1E 17 to 3A 22. (see Newport plan).

Tennyson Trail -1D 17 to 2B 14. (see Newport and Totland & Freshwater plans).

Worsley Trail -1C 22 to 3B 16. (see Shanklin plan).

## Monument / Folly

Earl of Yarborough Monument -2E 19. Obelisk (built 1849) in memory of the first Earl of Yarborough, founder of the Royal Yacht Squadron, who died in1846.

E.L.M. Monument NT -see Totland & Freshwater plan -5G.

Havenstreet War Memorial -4B 12. Walled enclosure with stone building, containing monument to 2nd Lieutenant Richard Willis-Fleming killed in Egypt in WW1, serving as a war memorial for the local parishes.

Hoy Monument -2D 21. 22 m (72 ft) high Alexandrian pillar on square base surmounted by finial sphere on St Catherine's Down. Erected by Michael Hoy in 1814 to commemorate the visit by Tsar Alexander I of Russia to Britain. Later adapted, rather incongruously, as a Crimean war memorial. Approached on footpath from Chale or Blackgang Viewpoint car park.

Marconi Memorial -2B 14. Stone with narrative plaques, at corner of Alum Bay car park, commemorating where Guglielmo Marconi carried out early experiments in long-distance radio telegraphy from the Needles Hotel to ships in the bay between 1897 & 1900.

Tennyson's Monument -2B 14. 12 m (40 ft) high granite iona cross erected in 1897 on clifftop of Tennyson Down 147 m (482 ft) above sea level, both a navigation beacon & a memorial to Victorian poet laureate Alfred, Lord Tennyson in one of his favourite spots. Fine views.

Worsley Obelisk -1F 21. Cornish granite obelisk (on plinth with 2 plaques attached) erected on Appuldurcombe Down in 1774 by Sir Richard Worsley of Appuldurcombe House in memory of his ancestor Sir Robert Worsley. Originally 21.3 m (70 ft) high, the obelisk was badly damaged by lightning in 1831 & restored as a shorter version in 1983.

## Museum

Bembridge Heritage Centre -see Bembridge plan -2A, S.

Blackgang Sawmill -3D 21, S Tel: 01983 730052 / 730330 / 730305. Story of wood set in a reconstructed watermill. Blacksmith, cooper & wheelwright workshop displays. Working steam & oil engines, mill cottage, timber at sea & timber at home displays. Mill pond gardens.

Brading Old Town Hall -see Brading plan -2B, S.

Brighstone Village Museum NT -3B 16, Tel: 01983 740689. Small Victorian themed village life museum, run by Brighstone Museum Trust, (& National Trust shop) in terrace of thatched Isle of Wight vernacular cottages.

Carisbrooke Castle Museum -see Newport plan -6C.

Classic Boat Museum, The -see Newport plan -2F, S.

Cowes Maritime Museum -see Cowes plan -3E.

Dinosaur Farm Museum -1B 20, S Tel: 01983 740401 /

07970 626456. Island fossil displays including part of brachiosaur dinosaur skeleton discovered on farm & excavated in 1992. One huge leg has been reconstructed. Conservation work can be viewed in progress.

Dinosaur Isle Museum, -see Sandown plan -2F.

Havenstreet Station Railway Museum -1B 18, S Tel: 01983 882204. Collection of small railway artifacts from the former railways on the Island. Signs, photographs, tokens, badges & block equipment.

Isle of Wight Bus & Coach Museum, -see Newport plan -2F, S.

Isle of Wight Military History Museum -3D 11, S. Military vehicles including Conqueror tank & Scammell on 6 ha. site of former Northwood Camp. Static exhibits, mobile demonstrations, military vehicle rides. Due open late 2001.

Isle of Wight Natural History Centre -4F 17, S Tel: 01983 840333. 17th century coach house housing shell room with over 40,000 shells from both tropical & local shores, & mineral room with fossils & minerals, precious & semi-precious stones & crystal replicas of the worlds most famous diamonds & how they were cut. Also 1953 crystal replicas of the Crown Jewels, animal room displaying stuffed animals & tropical fish aquarium.

Isle of Wight Shipwreck Centre & Maritime Museum (Bembridge Maritime Museum) -see Bembridge plan -2A, S.

Lilliput Antique Doll & Toy Museum, The -see Brading plan -2B.

Longshoreman's Museum -see Ventnor plan -3C, S.

Newport Guildhall Museum of Island History -see Newport plan -3F.

Nostalgia Toy Museum -4F 17, S Tel: 01983 840181. Large display of mostly post-war collectible toys & diecast models (mainly cars) dating from 1935 to 1970 by makers such as Dinky, Corgi & Matchbox.

Parkhurst Heritage Museum -4D 11, Tel: 01983 298756 / 853316. 1000's of items recalling Parkhurst Prison since 1838. Victorian equipment, strait-jackets, secretly made weapons, mug shots, punishment records, transportation to Australia. By appointment only.

Puckpool Park Wireless Museum -4D 13, S Tel: 01983 567665. Small volunteer run museum with displays of wireless & television receivers, transmitters & working crystal sets.

St Catherine's Quay -3D 21, S Tel: 01983 730052 / 730330 / 730305. The story of Blackgang's coast. 19th century quayside & warehouse scene. Shipwreck collection, 26.5 m (87 ft) whale skeleton (stranded here in 1845), Liverpool class RNLI lifeboat & display with models, paddle steamer engine room, coastal erosion exhibition & 19th century beach scene (with bathing machine).

Sir Max Aitken Museum -see Cowes plan -2E, S.

Smuggling History, The Museum of -3A 22, S Tel: 01983 853677. Smuggling methods over a 700 year period. 300 exhibits housed in three large underground galleries. Tableaux of events & personalities of the trade. Included are exhibits on ingenious ways of smuggling & things smuggled such as wool, brandy, silks, tobacco, tea, gold watches & diamonds.

Sunken History Exhibition -1C 14, S Tel: 01983 760283. Sea-bed archaeology & submerged settlements of the Solent. Stories of the discovery & excavation of the 16th century Venetian cargo ship Santa Lucia, wrecked off Yarmouth, & the transportation of convicts to Australia.

Swiss Cottage Museum, Osborne House EH -3F 11, S Tel: 01983 200022. Built in 1862 to house Queen Victoria's children's collections including geological specimens, shells, stuffed animals & birds, & foreign tour mementoes. The collection was initially housed in the sitting room of the

Swiss Cottage. Nearby is the Queen's bathing machine & the preserved deckhouse of the Royal Steam Yacht 'Alberta'.

**Timmy Taylor's Toy Box** -see Newport plan -3E.

**Ventnor Heritage Museum** -see Ventnor plan -2C, **S**.

**Yafford Mill Agricultural Museum -4B 16**, Tel: 01983 741125. Displays of old farm machinery, tractors, traction engine in 14.5 ha. grounds surrounding Yafford Mill. Ornamental waterfowl, rare breed cattle, jacob sheep & pigs. Owls & monkeys. 1 mile long nature walks by mill stream & through woodland.

## Natural Attraction

**Alum Bay -2B 14**. World famous multi-coloured sands in vertical bands. Named after the alum ore which was once mined here. (Access to the cliff face is discouraged as it is dangerously unstable).

**Blackgang Chine -3D 21**, **S**. A wide deep ravine mainly bare of vegetation rising to 122 m (400 ft) above Chale Bay on one of its flanks. The chine is subject to severe landslips at the junction of the dark blue/black gault clay (known as 'Blue Slipper') & layers of yellow sandstone. The chine was more spectacular in Victorian times when it extended some 320 m (350 yd) further towards the sea, & before the 1928 landslip at Windy Corner (to the south-east) which destroyed the Blackgang to Niton road.

**Landslip, The -2C 22**. Between Luccombe Chine & Dunnose Point, divided into Upper Landslip & Lower Landslip, accessed from The Landslip (Smugglers Haven) Picnic Site, Bonchurch or the top of Luccombe Chine. Paths wind through trees & undergrowth covering rocks & debris from the great landslip of 1810 (& those of 1928 & 1995) when the upper greensand geological bed slipped on the gault clay bed below in wet weather. Wishing Seat. The Devil's Chimney is a set of steep steps in a narrow ravine up to the main Leeson Road (366 m or 400 yd south of the picnic site).

**Luccombe Chine -2C 22**. Rough steps form a twisting path leading through dense undergrowth down the north side of the chine from the coastal path. The cove at the bottom was once used by smugglers, hence the belvedere tower for the Customs & Excise men in the grounds of the Luccombe Chine House hotel (private) above.

**Miniature Needles** -see Totland & Freshwater plan -5F.

**Needles, The -3A 14**. 3 famous chalk monoliths at the most westerly point of the Island, the ragged end of a chalk ridge which forms Tennyson & Compton Downs. A fourth needle between the first & third needles known as 'Lots Wife', at 37 m (121 ft), taller than the current lighthouse, fell into the sea in 1764.

**Shanklin Chine** -see Shanklin plan -4D, **S**.

**Shepherd's Chine -2B 20**. Well defined chine on the south-west coast of the Island. A steep sided gully cutting through the cliffs into Brighstone Bay crossed mid-way by the Shepherds Trail & the Isle of Wight Coastal Path.

**Whale Chine -2C 20**. Most spectacular of the chines on the south-west coast of the Island. A short steep sided narrow gully cutting through the cliffs into Chale Bay.

## Nature Reserve / Bird Sanctuary

See also Forest Walk

**Afton Marshes Local Nature Reserve** -see Totland & Freshwater plan -4F.

**Alverstone Mead Local Nature Reserve** -see Sandown plan -1A.

**America Wood Nature Reserve** -see Shanklin plan -2A.

**Dodnor Creek & Dickson's Copse Local Nature Reserve -4E 11**. 8.8 ha. reserve, formed from a former mill pond once associated with cement mills on the banks of the River Medina. Freshwater marshes, ponds & oak woodland (bisected by the Cowes-Newport cycleway). Breeding wetland birds.

**Eaglehead & Bloodstone Copses Nature Reserve -1C 18**. 6.9 ha chalk scarp woods comprising ash & hazel coppice. A public footpath traverses Eaglehead Copse & part of Bloodstone Copse; off this path the reserve is closed to the public.

**Mill Copse Nature Reserve** -see Yarmouth plan -2D.

**Newtown Harbour Nature Reserve NT -4A 10**. 338 ha. of mudflats, saltmarsh, & ancient woodland inhabited by red squirrels, forming the estuary of the Newtown River, amounting to 10 miles with all its branches; designated a national nature reserve in 1995. Nest site for black-headed gulls & overwintering wildfowl (such as Brent goose) & waders. In the 14th century this was the harbour for the once prosperous port of Newtown; the old quay is still extensively used for yacht moorings.

**Pelham Woods Nature Reserve -3A 22**. Wood on ancient boulder strewn St Lawrence landslip. Sycamore, English elm & hazel/ash scrub. Springs with alder growth. Largest & oldest oak tree on the Undercliff.

**Rew Down Local Nature Reserve** -see Ventnor plan -2A.

**Shide Chalk Pit Nature Reserve** -see Newport plan -5G.

**Youngwoods Copse Nature Reserve -2B 18**. Small oak wood with some silver birch. Understorey of holly & hazel. Wild service tree. Unimproved wet pasture to west.

## Picnic Site

*Blackgang Viewpoint Picnic Site -3D 21.*
*Brading Down Picnic Site -2C 18.*
*Firestone Copse Picnic Site, Havenstreet -4B 12.*
*Fort Victoria Country Park Picnic Site, Norton -1C 14.*
*Golden Hill Country Park Picnic Site, Freshwater -see Totland & Freshwater plan -1D.*
*Havenstreet Station Picnic Site -1B 18, S.*
*Landslip (Smugglers Haven) Picnic Site, The, Bonchurch -2C 22.*
*Medina Arboretum Picnic Site, Newport -see Newport plan -1F.*
*Medina Riverside Picnic Site, Newport -see Newport plan -1F.*
*Parkhurst Forest Picnic Site -see Newport plan -1B.*
*Puckpool Park Picnic Site, Spring Vale -4D 13.*
*St Helen's Church Picnic Site, St Helens -1E 19.*
*Tower Gardens Picnic Site, Shanklin -see Shanklin plan -4D.*
*Yarmouth Common Picnic Site -see Yarmouth plan -1D.*
*Yarmouth River Road Picnic Site -see Yarmouth plan -2C.*

## Place of interest (General)

**3D World** -see Brading plan -2B, **S**.

**Alum Bay Glass -2B 14**, **S** Tel: 01983 752401. Studio glassworks making coloured hand-blown decorative & functional glassware & jewellery including vases, bowls, ornaments & perfume bottles. Glassblowing demonstrations.

**Ashey Seamark, The -1B 18**. White triangular masonry seamark built in 1735 for navigation purposes. Once the site of a semaphore station relaying information on shipping movements off the Island to the admiralty at Portsmouth.

**Bembridge Lifeboat Station** -see Bembridge plan -2D.

**Chessell Pottery -2E 15**, Tel: 01983 531248. Pottery established in 1978 making hand made porcelain using designs based on the natural world, such as miniature water gardens, indoor fountains, fantasy animal figurines & decorative fish. The production process, from the preparation of the porcelain clay to the making, decorating & firing of the completed ware, may be observed in the studio workshops. A permanent technical & historical exhibit traces the materials, their geological origin, & manufacturing techniques as well as displaying historical product examples. Exhibition showroom. Children's 'clay-play' chalet.

**East Cowes Heritage Centre** -see Cowes plan -4F.

**Fort Victoria Model Railway -1C 14**, **S** Tel: 01983 761553. Largest & most advanced layout in Britain. German setting with over 330 buildings, 27 working models & 450 people at HO scale, Computer controlled, 25 trains per sequence (from a choice of 60) run over a continuous 143 m (470 ft) long main line.

**Freemantle Gate -1A 22**. Large arched ornamental gateway to Appuldurcombe Park built in the late 18th century to designs by James Wyatt & now reached by bridleway or footpath only. On Stenbury Trail & Worsley Trail.

**Glory Art Glass** -see Sandown plan -3D, **S**.

**Island Brass Rubbing Centre -2F 17**, **S** Tel: 01983 526290 / 527553. Brass rubbing of medieval copy brasses (knights in armour, costumed ladies & heraldic beasts) in Coach House adjacent to St George's Church. Metallic waxes & specialist papers are provided.

**Island Planetarium -1C 14**, **S** Tel: 01983 761555 / 0800 1958295. Small 32 seat planetarium with varying shows. Exhibition of working astronomical models & telescopes. Displays on current space exploration & amateur astronomy.

**Isle of Wight Glass -3F 21**, Tel: 01983 853526. Glassmaking studio (in converted barn) founded in 1973 by international glassmaker Michael Harris producing decorative & functional hand-blown glass in richly coloured designs using new techniques. Some designs such as Azurene use fused 22ct gold & sterling silver leaf, & as well as the standard collections, limited editions & one-off pieces are produced using techniques such as 'Graal' & multi-layered 'casing'. Glassmaking demonstrations (not weekends) by the studios ten glassmakers demonstrate the skilled stages involved in the production of the pieces.

**Isle of Wight Model Railways Exhibition** -see Cowes plan -2E.

**Isle of Wight Pearl -4F 15**, Tel: 01983 740352. Display of over 35,000 pieces of pearl jewellery using natural, cultivated & imitation pearls . Life size replica of world's largest natural pearl. Oyster tank.

**Isle of Wight Wax Works** -see Brading plan -2B.

**Model Village, The -4F 17**, **S** Tel: 01983 840270. Island life in miniature with stone houses (many with thatched roofs), gardens, 100's of dwarfed conifer trees, aircraft, boats, trains, cars & people set in the 0.6 ha. old vicarage gardens. 1/10th scale models of Godshill (complete with model of the model) & Shanklin Old Village & Chine set in the late 1930s. The original model village first opened to the public in 1952.

**Needles Park Chairlift -2B 14**, **S** Tel: 01983 752401. Chairlift from Needles Park to Alum Bay beach. Views of coloured sands.

**Pine Raft, The -3E 15**. Fossilised remains of tree trunks believed to be a log-jam from a primeval pine forest. Visible at low tide off Hanover Point.

**Ryde Pier** -see Ryde plan -2E.

**Sandown Pier** -see Sandown plan -4D.

**Shanklin Cliff Lift** -see Shanklin plan -4E, **S**.

**Waltzing Waters -4D 13**, Tel: 01983 811333. Aqua theatre-water, light & music show. Patterns of moving water synchronized with music.

**Winkle Street -2A 16**. Well known unspoilt photogenic row of stone & thatched cottages opposite the River Caul Bourne.

**Yarmouth Pier** -see Yarmouth plan -1C.

## Prehistoric Monument

**Devil's Punchbowl -2C 18**. Bronze age burial mound in hedgerow north of Newport Road. On Brading Down, opposite on the south side of the road, is a countryside interpretation panel.

**Long Stone, The -3F 15**. 4 m (13 ft) high sandstone pillar, & fallen stone, part of a Neolithic long barrow dating from c.2500 BC. Long barrows are rare on the Island.

**Tennyson Down Mortuary Enclosure NT** -see Totland & Freshwater plan -5D.

## Railway (Heritage, Narrow Gauge, Miniature)

**Isle of Wight Steam Railway -1B 18**, **S** Tel: 01983 884343 / 882204. 5 mile long standard gauge steam railway using Victorian & Edwardian engines & carriages. Journey from Smallbrook Junction (access by Island Line only) to Wootton, via Ashey (no vehicular access) & Havenstreet (the main operating base).

## Roman Remains

**Brading Roman Villa, The** -see Brading plan -4A, **S**.

**Newport Roman Villa** -see Newport plan -4F, **S**.

## Spot Height

**St Boniface Down 241 m (791 ft)** -see Ventnor plan -1D.

**St Catherine's Hill 237 m (778 ft) NT -3D 21**. Second highest point on the Island. One of the few places (together with St Catherine's Down immediately to the north) from which both the west & east extremities of the Island can be seen.

## Theme Park

See also Leisure Park

**Blackgang Chine -3D 21**, **S** Tel: 01983 730052 / 730330 / 730305. Over 16 ha. of clifftop gardens originally opened to the Victorian public in 1842 by the Dabell family. The children's leisure park (set in an overall smuggling theme) includes such attractions as Bodger the Badgers Fairground & Show, Rumpus Mansion, Wild West Town, Dinosaurland, Nurseryland (with gnomes!), Sleeping Beauty's Castle, Smugglers Ship, Pirate Adventure Fort, Water Force & a maze. Floodlit on summer evenings (July to early September until 10pm) with 1000's of coloured lights.

## Viewpoint (180 degree)

See also Viewpoint (360 degree)

*Blackgang Viewpoint -3D 21.*

*Bonchurch Down Viewpoint NT -2B 22.*

*Bonchurch Viewpoint -see Ventnor plan -1F.*

*Bouldnor Viewpoint -1D 15.*

*Brading Down Viewpoint -2C 18.*

*Carisbrooke Castle Viewpoint -see Newport plan -6C.*

*Culver Down Viewpoint, Bembridge NT -2E 19.*

*Fort Victoria Country Park Viewpoint, Norton -1C 14.*

*St Boniface Down Viewpoint, Ventnor NT -see Ventnor plan -1C.*

## Viewpoint (360 degree)

See also Viewpoint (180 degree)

**Appuldurcombe Down Viewpoint, Wroxall -1F 21.**
**Bembridge Down Viewpoint** NT **-2E 19.**
**Limerstone Down Viewpoint, Brighstone -3B 16.**
**Mottistone Down Viewpoint, Brighstone -3F 15.**
**St Catherine's Hill Viewpoint, Blackgang** NT **-3D 21.**
**Tennyson Down Viewpoint, Freshwater Bay** NT **-2B 14.**

## Vineyard

**Adgestone Vineyard -2C 18,** Tel: 01983 402503. The oldest vineyard on the Island, established in 1968 on a 4 ha. south facing slope. Walks around the different grape varieties being grown & guided tours of the winery cellars where the making & bottling of wines is described. Pony & trap rides (afternoons, weather permitting).
**Morton Manor Vineyard** -see Brading plan -4A, S.
**Rosemary Vineyard** -see Ryde plan -7E.

## Visitor Centre / Information Centre

**Isle of Wight Coastal Visitors' Centre** -see Ventnor plan -3D.
**Newtown Harbour Nature Reserve Visitor Centre -4A 10.** Interpretation panels & exhibits on Newtown Harbour Nature Reserve.

**Shanklin Chine Heritage Centre** -see Shanklin plan -4D, S.
**Ventnor Botanic Garden Visitor Centre -3A 22,** Tel: 01983 855397. Opened in spring 2000 the centre has two exhibition areas comprising interactive displays on global issues & mans' link with plants, & a temporary exhibition area. The innovative building (entered from the car park) is designed as a series of linked pavilions cascading down the slope to a lower level.
**Whippingham St Mildred's Church Centre -3E 11,** S Tel: 01983 292130. Permanent exhibition associated with Whippingham St Mildred's Church containing a replica of Princess Beatrice's wedding dress, royal photographs, pictures & architect's drawings of the three churches which have existed on this site. Orchard picnic area.

## Windmill

See also Industrial Monument
**Bembridge Towermill** NT -see Bembridge plan -4A, S.

## Zoo / Safari Park

See also Animal Collection, Farm Park
**Isle of Wight Zoo & Jack Corney's Tiger & Big Cat Sanctuary** -see Sandown plan -2F.